Life *in my* Hands

Healing Myself, Healing Others

DARCY HOTCHKISS

Published by: WAT-AGE Publishing

ISBN: 978-0-9906343-4-8 (sc)
ISBN: 978-0-9906343-3-1 (e)

rev. date: 10/25/2016

Contents

Dedication

This book is dedicated to my daughter Jordan. You have been an enormous source of inspiration in my life. I'm amazed and proud of the young lady you have become, full of wisdom and compassion. May you always know the truth of who you are, never forget where you came from, and always continue to look forward, inspired and never too tired to go after your wildest dreams now and forever – Love, Mom.

To my parents, thank you for always telling me I could be anything in this life. Because of that I have become all sorts of things. Without all those things I would not be who I am today, I love you all.

To all the non-conventionalists, misfits, one-offs, wild hearts, black sheep, outcasts, free thinkers, rainmakers, do-gooders, firewalkers, warriors, trailblazers, creators, bizarros and weirdos, loners, rejects, odd ducks, eccentrics, paradigm crashers, slayers of nay-sayers and fearless challengers; may you continue on with your passion and electric bliss because this world really needs you.

Disclaimer

This book is creative nonfiction. Most events, persons and conversations were condensed from journals kept during my travels over the last twenty years. Conversations and events have been translated in the spirit, essence and intent of, and to the best of my memory. All of the events in this book are true, although some names and identifying details may have been altered to protect the privacy of those involved. Any health-based information noted in this book does not take the place of professional medical advice. Energy healing is a non-medical healing approach and does not diagnose or take the place of professional medical treatments.

Preface

Life in My Hands; Healing Myself, Healing Others is the story of my life. It isn't a story of great triumph or overcoming hellacious odds. It's a story of the unique and interesting way my life unfolded and ultimately healed. It's about the adventures of life I had with others; who and what made the biggest impacts and changed me forever.

Many people have written great stories about their lives. This one is mine about claiming myself and walking in a way that feels most peaceful and authentic to my being. When I began, I never understood how cathartic it would be to write this down and share my feelings with the world. Some days it felt freeing to get all these things about my life down on paper, and other days it felt like the most difficult and terrifying task in the world. I learned that facing myself was about accepting, loving, and honoring who I am. In order to do that, I needed to let go of the judgments that I had been taking on. Doing that wasn't an easy task, either. How do you refrain from judging yourself and others? I often found that difficult to do if I had something to defend. Part of me kept defending aspects of myself that resulted from the life I had led. The identity that I had created was of a strong, successful, smart woman who was on the top of everything and always had to get it right. Other labels were inherited: my father's daughter, a divorcee (twice), soldier, and eventually the healer. There are many more labels that I had given myself as well. In order to rest easy I had to be willing to see myself without all those creations. The truthful me doesn't rely on those important identifiers and has nothing to defend or concede. Especially with those who didn't meet the mark of my judgmental thresholds of good, bad, and so-so.

Doing healing work has been an important part of my evolution because it taught me to see divine in others whether they are at their best or worst. I learned to stay in the truth of who I am so that they could see the truth of who they are. The truth of who they are is not a depressed, sad, or one with arthritis or back pain. The truth of who they are is the divine Being that they forgot to reclaim each day because they were distracted by their illness.

I still don't have life figured out. Every time I think I do, it's like the rug gets yanked out from underneath me. I think I somehow expected to discover, figure out, or understand life better if I wrote this book, and laid it all out. Instead of making sense of things I may have just managed to uncover more I don't understand and deeper aspects of myself that hadn't yet come to the surface. What I do have today is a greater appreciation for the power of the human mind, body and spirit. There is a better sense of who I am and a keener realization of when I am just a bit too far out of my personal integrity. I understand more about how to honor and embrace parts of myself that feel vulnerable, and I've learned to love life more than I ever have before.

This is my story,

Darcy

Introduction

When I moved to the Middle East after my second marriage ended, my journey of self-discovery was just beginning. Did two failed marriages mean that I wasn't suited for that life? If so, what was my life meant to be?

I hungered for adventure, possibly as a way to trade my old life for a more interesting reality, while also hoping to escape the painful shadows of my past. I was ready to embrace a more purposeful, exciting, and satisfying existence, where I could achieve success. Reaching my goal, however, was not easy. Along the way, I would encounter psychological, emotional, and physical challenges. Through determination those obstacles were turned into stepping stones that helped me rise above some difficult situations.

Life in My Hands is my story, my journey of self-discovery. This is not just about overcoming obstacles in life. It's also about stepping into and embracing who we truly are at our core, while learning what it means to live a rich and dynamic life. In order for me to begin doing this in my life, I had to take responsibility for all the ways I was not yet doing it. It required that I stop feeling disadvantaged from my past and fearful of my future. Taking responsibility was a way to eliminate the gap between what my life was and what I dreamed it could be.

I hope as you read about my experiences, you will reflect on your own. Don't be afraid to jot down your own thoughts in the margins! There were opportunities along the way in my journey where I may have been able to do things better had I known better. Can you relate? While you may not be able to go back and correct past mistakes (heaven only knows, I tried and failed), you might glean strategies to discover the silver lining in situations, allowing movement in a useful direction.

My life has never lacked for drama — first as a pregnant teenager dropping out of high school, then as a single mother living on welfare, and eventually joining the United States Army where I hoped I could change my life forever. Military life was challenging, but I learned to trust my own abilities and found I was capable of more than I had ever thought possible. That realization was empowering and helped to fuel my future growth.

My career took me to Europe and while I was climbing the professional ladder, my physical and emotional health suffered. After exhausting what traditional medicine had to offer, I discovered a nonconventional approach to healing that, quite simply, saved my life. As a result of my own healing, I was inspired to become a healer myself. The act of healing others has added immeasurably to my own journey since I learn something new each time I work with a client.

In chapter ten, I explain how I was led to finding resolution, but not before my trouble was compounded by an unfortunate accident. One night, teetering on fashionable but too-high heels, I took a terrible fall down a set of ladder-like treacherous Dutch stairs. I was already living with deep emotional pain. After that fall, I added severe and chronic physical pain that took over and quickly consumed my life. Being in constant physical pain for over eight months seemed like an indictment that would never end. The drawn out recovery process was a catalyst that prompted me to take personal inventory of what my life had become. I found myself asking again, where do I fit in? What am I doing? Why am I here enduring this life? I was led to perilously questioning my life to a depth like never before. I began by reviewing aspects of how I was living, and trying to understand the motivators behind all my choices that seemed to lead me to a place I didn't really want to be.

While on bed rest I came across a number of videos describing various types of alternative healing. For thousands of years, Eastern medicine has successfully harnessed the use of prana, chi, ki, life force energy, or simply "energy," for its culture's healing. Today, Western cultures are starting to recognize the value in many ancient healing modalities, and how they can be used to reverse various illnesses. Curiously enough, these ancient healing practices are being called "New Age."

My inquisitiveness led me to deep dive into researching energy techniques and healers. While many things found were impressive, I had some initial skepticism because it seemed almost too easy, too good to be true. Later that skepticism and curiosity would lead me to uncover an even bigger personal discovery and mission that would involve elements of this work as its foundation.

It seemed I had been searching most of my life to uncover certain timeless truths; my personal truth or even just some kind of "happyish" balance. The illusive happiness seemed like a collateral result of the hard and sometimes bold decisions that I had to make in order to get through life. Although I've made many difficult, and some would even say, bad choices along the way, there has been healing in this journey. These choices that led me to the good, the bad, and everything in between, all needed to happen in order for me to be who I am today. Having searched for a way to address the unresolved issues every step of the way, it felt like the personal tragedies and pieces of my life falling apart were necessary in order for everything to fall into place.

Many life lessons have been learned along my trek. We all struggle with love, for ourselves and for each other. The result of my work has helped me find that love for myself again. It has not only healed me, but also many of my clients. I discovered that the heart is the center of each person's being, so I found myself helping each client to heal emotionally as well as physically. Along the way, I also learned how to face and resolve the pain in my own heart. At the core of our being is the heart, acting as a receiver, a beacon of communication from our soul. When pain in the heart is resolved, clarity of the messages and alignment with life's higher purposes and truth can be recognized. The mastery of life seems to unfold much easier, with less resistance and fewer struggles.

Witnessing remarkable transformations in others has been a humbling experience. I realized how my big brontosaurus-sized ego claimed so much responsibility for things that really had nothing to do with me. In my heart, I know that the healing I'm facilitating is far from my doing.

The fact that it's all happening through me has been the most transformational thing I've ever personally observed, and has profoundly changed the way I view illness, wellness, and other imbalances in life. What it really feels like is that I am witnessing a higher order of work every time I touch someone, and how could anyone claim credit for that?

Healing work teaches, and those coming to me for help astonishingly mirrored some of my own past struggles. In fact sometimes they acted as a glaring spotlight on the closure that had been missed and reminded me of the extra weight I had been carrying emotionally. I lived with depression and emotional pain for years after leaving the Middle East. I kept searching for answers, wanting to be better, never understanding why happiness was so elusive, and never once dreaming that the answers to my challenges would unfold in the way they did.

Life felt like a blindfolded game of bumper cars, as if I was getting hit from all directions, without a charted course. In time, I matured, healed, and maybe even became a little enlightened along the way. The search for my own personal evolution charted a new course. What an excellent odyssey it has been!

CHAPTER 1

The Beginning

"Don't ever let someone tell you that you can't do something. Not even me. You got a dream, you gotta protect it. When people can't do something themselves, they're gonna tell you that you can't do it. You want something, go get it. Period."

—Will Smith (as Chris Gardner)
The Pursuit of Happyness (Film)

I love the journey of my life. Up to this point it has been extremely rich. While living and working abroad, I traveled all around Europe and the Middle East. Along the way, I experienced great upset and gut-wrenching heartbreak, as well as moments of complete and blissful peace. I witnessed and participated in healing miracles happening before my eyes.

Just to be up front, I don't really think I'm anyone special. I don't see myself as a gifted person. (I'm sure my mother would disagree!) I am a normal, curious person having an extraordinary experience in this lifetime.

It didn't start out that way, though. I grew up in rural Maine, in a small town that was one of three or four that made up one school district. My high school class had less than 100 students. Although my parents divorced when I was very young, they both worked very hard to support the family. We weren't rich, but we always had what we needed and were taught to appreciate and make do with what we had. If we wanted more, we were told to work harder. I grew up spending the summers riding my bike around the neighborhood until the street lights came on, walking down long country roads to visit friends, camping and swimming at the lake, and playing in lush green woods until just after sunset. Growing up in small town Maine made for a priceless childhood in many ways. I was completely unaware that we lived in what was considered an economically depressed area. As a kid, I enjoyed and valued the intangibles, which created my best memories and continue to stay with me even today.

A lot of the younger generation in my town moved away for college or to pursue different opportunities and experiences. I moved away, too. I got pregnant, married at 17, and quit high school. I ended up spending the next three or four years struggling to get by, barely making ends meet.

Shortly after attending my junior prom, I discovered I was pregnant. The idea of becoming a parent was overwhelming. I was facing something much bigger than myself, but had no idea how big. There were times when I felt supported and happy, mostly because my long-term boyfriend (later my husband) was really excited.

The physical reality of my condition soon became apparent with persistent morning sickness and my body transforming into something I could barely recognize. In my eighth month of pregnancy, I stood behind a cash register at the local grocery store, working as many hours as possible, trying to save money while I still had the ability to work. With my back and feet aching, and my ankles swollen like russet potatoes, I was also confronted with a realization that terrified me: I was going to be responsible for another human life. It would be my job to ensure that this little person would grow to be a productive member of society. This was the scariest realization yet, aside from the realization that eventually the baby would actually come out of me. I had no idea what to expect of the whole process. At times, my thoughts terrified me. How were we going to do this? I was a cashier who hadn't even finished high school. Looking back, that was a turning point. My terror proved to be the catalyst for my transformation into someone ready to take on the responsibilities of being a parent.

My parents, naturally, were mortified by my news. I now understand that they were afraid for me, knowing that there was no turning back, and that I still had no clue what I was taking on. They knew because they had become parents when they were very young. History repeats itself, one generation to the next. Getting pregnant before having the emotional and financial resources to cope is a tough road to hoe. Like my parents, my husband and I never understood what challenges lay ahead until we were already living it out.

During my early years as a new parent, my family, my extended family, and my close friends were silently shaking their heads either in pity or disapproval, or maybe both. Not once did I feel that I had let myself down, regardless of what others thought. I truly felt that our daughter, Jordan, was meant to be in our lives. I believe that nothing in life is an accident. Whether we understand it or not, there is always a divine plan. Of course, I did feel at a disadvantage at times, especially early on. Having a child at such a young age was challenging. Having to pay for food, diapers, and daycare while earning minimum wage often meant that one of us went without. My social life took a hit. While my friends were enjoying the beach, going to the senior prom, and drinking at house parties, I was at home, a wife and mother with responsibilities. I didn't spend those years with my peers and I didn't walk at my high school graduation, either. But there are no regrets about what was missed, because I know now what was gained from having my daughter. While pregnant, I finished high school by taking evening classes and summer courses. I received my high school diploma just a couple of months after our daughter was born.

Jordan was tiny and fragile and we were completely terrified. Since we had never read anything by Dr. Spock, I'm quite certain we made many mistakes. By the time my daughter turned one, I was overwhelmed with being a wife and raising a child. My husband and I had completely different goals and ideas about what our lives would be, certainly a challenge to our relationship. I wanted a career, and to travel and see the world, while he wanted to stay on the farm, raise children, and be the softball coach and team dad. He didn't understand why being at home wasn't enough for me. I didn't understand how his idea of life could ever be enough for him. Predictably, our marriage began to crumble. By year three we were fully separated and nearly divorced.

Today, I understand that beyond raising a child as a teenager, being a partner or a wife is also a very complex undertaking. I didn't possess the emotional maturity, or the problem-solving and communication skills. I couldn't figure out how to hold onto a vision of myself, while also fulfilling my duties as a wife and mother. As teenagers, my husband and I didn't have enough "practice" or development in those areas that would allow us to succeed as a married couple. We did not take time to discuss and understand what each of us really wanted in life. If we had engaged in those discussions upfront, we might have chosen a different path.

We did love each other, but perhaps we were overly optimistic that a union could succeed despite our polar opposite personalities, life goals, and perspectives. The marriage may have been doomed from the beginning, but as parents, we gave our daughter one of the most dynamic upbringings she could have ever experienced.

Despite a few rocky months after our separation, we quickly came together and worked to create an "all about Jordan" relationship in our interactions. Right from the beginning, we agreed that no matter what followed or how our lives moved on, Jordan's interest would always come first.

When the divorce was finalized, I moved from his family's farm and back into my hometown, where I received public assistance, including public housing, food stamps, and welfare. My family's resources were limited, and I didn't feel comfortable asking them for help. After all, it was my job to create a life for Jordan and myself, not theirs. The statistics for single teenage mothers making great lives for themselves and their children were not in my favor, and I knew the road ahead was going to be a difficult one. I needed to create a better situation for my daughter and myself. There was no bail out coming for me and I had no expectation for one. Of course, I wasn't the only one struggling in my small town. Everywhere I looked, there were others fighting for survival. Was I different? Perhaps. I knew that I was meant to live a bigger life. My restlessness kept me unsettled, constantly thinking about seeing the world and having an exciting career. That life was the one I was meant to live, not barely scraping by "surviving" or being tossed in the welfare bin with the rest of the divorced single mothers on public assistance. This fire burning inside of me was not easy to explain to those around me. I was consumed with a passion for something beyond what I could see, something that was exciting, expansive, freeing, and positive. The life I envisioned was the opposite of my life with Jordan in my little town.

From my earliest memory as a child, when I closed my eyes and imagined my life as a grown up, I always saw myself traveling, flying across the oceans, and living internationally. I saw myself wearing business clothes and being successful, as a leader, a teacher, speaking on stages in front of large audiences. Physically, I saw myself as a runner. I always loved to run and would tell people, "When I grow up I want to be a runner." Running made me feel free and alive, and in some way it came to symbolize all the other images that would appear when my eyes were closed — the plane, the fancy clothes, the stage, etc. Those things didn't fit into the box of anything else I'd ever seen growing up. No one around me had the career and professional life I kept seeing for myself. Little did I know that these thoughts and ideas I was seeing in my mind would actually become part of my life's work later on, a career that would take me to places near and far, an epic journey that would become my life.

One thing became clear: if I ever wanted to make those visions a reality, I needed to find a way to leave my small town. The timing was not great. Not only was the economy bad, my resume was lacking. I had very little education, and barely graduated high school. I was living on public assistance and food stamps, working minimum wage jobs. Living in public housing and seeing people around me who had spent years struggling in the same situation created a clear indication that, as long as we were there, we were going to be trapped in an endless poverty cycle. I had to find a way out. I didn't want my daughter to grow up with public housing as her highest standard of living. I'm not judging people who need that assistance, but I wanted more for myself and for my daughter. To me, public assistance was supposed to be a stepping-stone to the beginning of a much bigger journey. It had to be, because my ex-husband and I owed her more than the life I was able to give her at that time. In my mind, I was letting her down by not giving her the best chance for a wonderful life, due to a situation she had no part in creating.

I made the most difficult choice that a single mother could make — I joined the Army. While going through basic training, my daughter, then four years old, went to live with her father. I endured even more criticism from people around me. What kind of a mother was she? What kind of mother leaves her child? That judgment and disapproval from friends and family was mostly silent, but still sharp and injurious. I felt the disapproval when people looked at me. Years later, I still dealt with the guilt of leaving her with her dad while moving away to get my life together.

A couple of weeks before I was set to ship off, I nearly backed out. My Army recruiter showed up with the declination (DEC) statement that would absolve me from the obligation I had signed with the Army. Staff Sergeant Lewis was a salty guy from South Boston, and he said, "Look kid, if you want to do this or you don't, I don't really care. Just sign here, right now, and press hard because you're making two copies. Go right back to your normal life. But if you don't make some kind of a change, you're going to look back in ten years and be in the same place you are now, and you've said you don't want that. I don't care what you do, but you need to have a plan to get out of here, or do something else. You have so much more potential than what you are doing." I didn't sign the DEC statement that day. "No, I'm going, I'm doing this." I told him, "This is my ticket out of here." I would join the Army again, a hundred times over. In fact, the only thing that I would change is that I would have done it sooner. The Army was the best choice for me and for my daughter, regardless of what people thought. At the time, I was not the best parent I could be for my daughter, and I knew that. Her father was the best parent, and he still is a great father. Being with him at that time was in her very best interest. I could never have gone on this journey without his support and his family's help in raising our daughter. I will always be grateful to him and his wife for that.

Friends and family were confused about my plan. Some asked, "Why would you want to do this?" Others wanted to know "What's your back-up plan just in case you fail?" There was no back up plan, and there was no plan B, because there was no way I was going back to that situation. Failure was simply not an option. I did have my doubts and fears. What if this decision was terrible and what if I didn't like it? What if it was unbearable? I told myself, "Well, you will learn to like it until you can create another opportunity out of it, or something else comes up." By and large, I was going down this path, armed with faith, and intuition, somehow knowing that things would go my way. I had to take this opportunity ultimately to create a better life for us both.

Joining the Army was a major stretch for me emotionally and mentally. It pushed my boundaries. I remember how much confidence and trust I felt after completing basic training. The scary leap was taken, and as it turned out, I didn't fail. I didn't even hate it and found the experience neither terrible nor unbearable. There was an adjustment period to the military culture, of course, but even with that period of adapting, I found the transition personally fulfilling. I became aware of my true level of strength, what could be accomplished, and how powerful my mental attitude really was. Essentially, I got to see what I was made of and realized that I was not only strong and physically capable, but also mentally tough and could literally do anything that I set my mind to do. Big tasks looked insurmountable and difficult, but once starting down a path, I found that things weren't as complicated as I thought. I learned that success depended on having the right mindset and approach, consistently facing each task with perseverance and discipline. No one had ever told me this before, and I had never been pushed to the edge emotionally and physically in that way. It was a major turning point in my life, but it was still just the beginning.

There are a lot of things that can be said about the military and how serving in the military affects people. There are positive and negative aspects to everything we pursue in life. For me, the military was a positive experience overall. I took whatever was useful and good from my experience and forgot the rest that didn't work. I went through a transformation with each week of basic training. I not only increased my level of physical fitness, but also gained more mental and emotional agility, which fostered a higher level of confidence and belief in my own self-worth and personal abilities. At some point in the program, I started to think basic training was almost easier than my life back home. I got more sleep than I did as a single mother jockeying college classes, homework, work, and spending time with my daughter. There was no longer a need to make decisions about when to pay rent to avoid a bounced check. I didn't need to decide if the electric and water bill should be let go a bit longer so I could buy groceries instead. I certainly wasn't seeking a second or third job on the weekends cleaning apartments for extra money. My life became less complicated in some ways and the stress of survival was gone.

Halfway through basic training, we were being pushed and played with by the drill sergeants. One ordered us to run from one side of a football field to another and regroup into new formations at his order. The other would then call "fall in" from another side of the field. We'd all run to the other side to get into a new formation, and then rinse, lather, and repeat. The drill went on over and over again for what seemed like hours. We were all exhausted. I could see my peers getting angry and frustrated, and begin to bicker with each other. This, of course, only turned up the heat from the drill sergeants, and they began increasing the tempo to the point where we were just running back and forth nonstop. When someone would fall out in the back, we would have to start again. We reached a time when we all just stopped questioning the purpose of the exercise because we understood that they were training us not to question orders, but just to follow what was being asked of us.

Something clicked inside of me during these endless drills. Following orders without questioning? Oh boy! This is going to be tough if I have to spend a career blindly following orders. Some people need to be questioned to be kept accountable. But during basic training, I went with the flow, kept my mouth shut, and followed the program. I reminded myself that basic training lasted only ten weeks. Even if they had us running back and forth for the next ten weeks, I knew I could do anything for just ten weeks. Lots of people had done these exercises before me. I wasn't the first one and I wouldn't be the last. The drill sergeants had no idea that I came from a very long line of seriously stubborn genetic stock. So when it was my turn to run back and forth or do whatever ridiculous thing they asked me to do, I played the game with glee and a smile. I faced every other suck fest they gave us in training with this same attitude. If they pushed me hard, I pushed myself harder, and smiled while doing it. This attitude inside of me started to rise to the surface: I'll follow the orders, but you won't control my point of view or spirit while I do what I'm being ordered to do. Playing the game was only hard if I believed it was hard and didn't realize it was just a game. I also began to see that my body would do whatever my mind dictated so I approached everything with a mind-over-matter mindset and always tried to keep myself in good mental spirits.

The senior drill sergeant yelled at me more than once to "wipe that grin off your face." I did a lot of extra push-ups and sand pit drills because of my smile. At the end of basic training, he said, "Private, you have been grinning at me this whole cycle." After the graduation he awarded me the banner from the platoon guidon for demonstrating the most motivation. I'm not sure whether I was, in fact, the most motivated, but I was pretty darn determined to get through it because there was no way I was going back to where I had come from.

Thinking about the experience today, I recognize that most every challenge or pain anyone faces on this journey is only temporary. Things always seem more complicated before you begin. Even if it is difficult, it too shall pass, as nothing lasts forever. When all was said and done and the dust settled on that part of my life, those challenges just became part of what I went through to transition to a more self-confident and self-assured person. Perhaps that was the intent of the training all along and I was a good student that learned to adapt and play well. Regardless, the basic training process made me aware that I was far more physically and mentally capable of doing something that I only suspected I might be able to do, and that I'm capable of even going beyond. Somewhere early on in life I got the silly idea that I couldn't trust in myself to be strong and accomplish things. There was a disempowering belief in me that I needed something or someone to rely on. Being a part of this training environment really gave me back the self-assured sense of who I am. A bold understanding of what I'm capable of doing was gained in this process; in retrospect it was all just an exercise of mind over matter.

CHAPTER 2

Mind over Matter

"What the mind can conceive, the body can achieve."
— Napoleon Hill

Some of the biggest obstacles that I have faced in my life have been ones that I've created. Essentially, I just needed to get over myself. I used to feel that I needed to control exactly how things would happen or unfold in my life. I quickly learned that if I just focused on holding the image of the desired outcome in my mind, the obstacles in my life would essentially disappear. As a single mother, I often envisioned a better life. Even though I was living in a less than desirable situation, I knew that what I was seeing could still come to pass. It was the "how to" aspect that often overwhelmed me and created stress. Yet, each night before falling asleep, these visualizations and images would appear. I saw myself successful and happy, with my daughter, all grown up, also successful and happy. I never saw the "how to" in the visualizations, and never dreamed that the path to get there would lead me through Army basic training and eventually the Middle East. Sometimes the "how to" isn't the most important part; just seeing the outcome as a possibility is enough to get started.

Before basic training, I had not done much physical activity in over seven years. I was active growing up, but nowhere near the most athletic amongst my peers. After Jordan was born, keeping the weight off became a battle. Working long hours, going to school, and taking care of my daughter as a single parent meant that I was lucky to get four to five hours of sleep a night. If there was any free time in my schedule, going to the gym wasn't my top priority.

On the first day of basic training, I could not even do a single push up. After I barely finished a two-mile run gasping for breath, I regretted the years I spent smoking and avoiding exercise. I began to wonder if joining the Army was the right choice. I knew it would be tough, but the reality of just how hard hit me like a ton of bricks. There was no time for a pity party, though. I knew I had to get my emotions and my mind in the right place, and quickly. Falling out of a run or failing a physical fitness test would be a black mark against me, as well as one of the most socially unacceptable things I could do in that environment. So, every night before I went to sleep, lying in my rack with my eyes closed, I would go through each part of the physical fitness test and see myself passing each event with ease. I visualized great physical fitness scores way before I achieved them. This strategy was also used days before entering the gas chamber training as well. The gas chamber is a room filled with a controlled concentration of CS (orto-chlorobenzylidene-malononitrile) gas, also known as tear gas. It's similar to what's in mace and capable of producing stinging eyes and inflamed sinuses. Imagine being in a small 12x12 enclosed room completely filled with CS, so full that it looks worse than a foggy day in London. It's as unpleasant as it sounds, more so for those who are claustrophobic.

To prepare myself emotionally and mentally for the gas chamber, I saw myself calmly moving through each task. Once in the room, the drill sergeants had us remove our gas masks, recite our names and social security numbers, as well as the "Soldiers Creed," then replace our masks and clear the room. On the day of the training, I was relaxed, maybe because I had already done this exercise in my mind several times before, or maybe because I had dealt with what would happen on an emotional level.

As we waited in line like cattle, some of the soldiers in my squad started to get nervous. The soldier ahead of me vomited even before we entered the holding area to the chamber. Soon it was our turn to step into the room. The door swung open and a puff of CS gas rolled out the doorway as we filed into the small building. People beside me were beginning to freak out. I could hear choking and coughing. A few were beginning to panic as the drill sergeants pressed them to move through their tasks faster. They were asked to recite the same information over and over again without their masks on. One soldier ran for the door, but a drill sergeant blocked his exit. A few soldiers, overtaken by anxiety, were unable to control their breathing, thus inhaling even more CS gas. While the sting of CS gas in the eyes was brutal, that feeling paled when compared to how the deep inhales of CS gas felt in the lungs. The only way to minimize the effect of the gas was to keep calm and breathe as shallowly as possible, as we were instructed to do. This drill was the least fun activity in the whole training, yet necessary for learning how to keep cool and follow steps under pressure.

The drill sergeant stepped over to me as I moved through each of the tasks, removing my mask, reciting everything that was asked of me. A little anxiety was starting to creep in, but I didn't want to prolong the exercise. The drill sergeant stared at me for a moment to see if I was shaken or uneasy. I think they got a bit of joy out of exploiting those who were squeamish. Keeping my breathing as shallow as possible, I gazed back at him without flinching and said to myself, "Wow this is easy, so easy, and I can do this all day, as long as you need me to." He finally nodded his head and told me to replace the gas mask. Staying calm, I slowly replaced the mask and tightened the straps around the outer edges. I placed the palm of my hand over the canister and then cleared the remaining CS gas from the inside of my mask. My eyes were burning and I was dying to take a deep breath of fresh air. We weren't out of the woods yet, and my breathing still needed to be controlled until we were allowed to go outside. I could see the drill sergeants looking for those who were still panicked. They were being asked to remove their masks again. Once the training was completed, we formed a line at the exit and, one by one, were allowed to walk out of the chamber. Although my discomfort was growing, I kept my emotions in check and walked out of the gas chamber training with just a memory of having a very runny nose and really clear sinuses afterward. The drill could have gone much worse for me if I wasn't able to keep it together. There were times in my life where I've panicked. But this time out, being prepared mentally helped me remain emotionally stable.

During training, I didn't know that what I was doing was called visualization, a pretty common tool used by a lot of successful people. I'm sure if I tried to explain it then, people would have thought I was nuts, but this visualization work became my nightly ritual. Before dozing off, I would visualize how the next day's challenging event would enfold. Even today, before falling asleep I spend time seeing my life how I want it to be, as opposed to obsessing over the negative or unwanted aspects that may be present. It's an exercise in mental conditioning, mind over matter.

When people refer to mind over matter, they are talking about the ability to surpass the obstacle, physical matter, or a physical manifestation of a situation (reality) using the power of the mind. Mind over matter is usually referenced when people are talking about overcoming insurmountable odds or situations with focused mental effort or good old fashion relentlessness. This is nothing more than using creative thought energy to create a desired outcome; it's similar to daydreaming. Creative thought energy is the energy behind imagination; this coincides with the idea that if you can conceive it, you can achieve it. A person's thoughts can and do affect physical matter. Matter is a physical manifestation of energy. Energy, as in the universal cosmic stuff all around us, makes up the Universe. It's life itself, known in other ancient cultures as chi, prana, or ki. It's the life force energy that is the essence of our very existence. There's plenty of science that has, at the very least, supported the theory that no object is actually solid, rather just rapidly moving atoms (matter), and therefore "energy" creating a solid-like state. If we understand fundamentally that everything is energy, including our thoughts, emotions, and the table that my laptop sits on as I type this, then we can start to expand our thinking about how we see every single object, person, and situation around us in a new light of fluid possibilities. If everything is just energy, then the idea of being able to affect energy (even physical matter) is just a new possibility. What if it's possible to tap into the energy of matter and move an object without touching it? Or change a situation by harnessing the energy in creative thought, thereby creating a new outcome? Or even use this energy to heal someone, whether that malady is serious, like a life threatening illness, or something minor, like a painful hangnail. There are many possible ways that this exchange of energy can affect daily life, even without understanding energy or being aware of what is happening.

People who practice mind over matter and visualization are tapping into sacred knowledge that's vanished from the mainstream and lost by many ancient societies. The Tibetan monks and Indian Yogis have the ability to manipulate processes within their bodies while in deep trances and meditative states. They have been known to bring their core body temperatures higher in a colder climate and slowing down their heart rates to a point where only an EKG machine and other scientific measurement tools are able to detect them. They are affecting their own physical state (matter) with their mind. These cases are extraordinary ones that require a bit of practice to achieve. Nonetheless, it's an example of how powerful the human mind is when harnessing and focusing energy.

There are many examples of how well-known Olympic medalists such as Michael Phelps and professional athletes like Michael Jordan utilize visualization and imagery (more creative thought energy) by playing out the game or swimming the meet in their mind, exactly how they would do it on the day of competition, homing in exactly the way that they want to perform on competition day, over and over again, to reach their desired goals.

Visualization or guided imagery is the simplest example of practicing mind over matter. No matter what your personal situation is, visualization provides the sense of empowerment needed to maintain a positive outlook towards achieving your goal. When imagining an outcome, you are directing your heart and mind (energy) toward your positive desire, and the new possibilities of how it could be, versus dwelling and harping on how terrible and how helpless you feel with the current situation, or doing what I call "worst case scenario gaming." There are always a hundred ways things can go right, just like there are always a hundred ways things can go wrong. You can choose how you experience life as it unfolds. With visualization, you're simply choosing the way to focus the attention (energy) in order to get the outcome you most desire. Attention is the currency of the Universe; you get what you want, based on your "paying" attention to it. Positive visualization creates emotional resiliency by establishing a sense of control, promotes and supports positive beliefs, and gives people a productive self-empowered way to manage stressful situations.

The human brain can never fully understand all the possibilities that are within reach. We can't always know exactly how our desired outcome will unfold and visualization creates new energetic pathways and possible outcomes. Without a catalyst for the new path, we didn't see the options previously. It's like learning a new way to get home after you have driven the same route for years. You didn't even know that route existed until a detour forced you to explore a new street. There was a bit of uncertainty and unfamiliarity along that path, but once you got to the destination, you realized it was easier and maybe more pleasurable, and the next day when you drove that same new route again and over time it too became familiar and easy. Now you have more than one path to get to where you want to go, either is fine, as long as you get to your destination.

There have been numerous scientific studies developed by pioneers in the imagery field. For example, The Job-Loss Recovery Program® was developed after a study done by Dr. Lynn Joseph to test the effectiveness of a guided imagery-based career transition program in workers who had lost their jobs. The program achieved higher return rates for the dislocated workers who went back to full-time employment and also were able to put the previous job loss in perspective. More than five times the study participants in the guided imagery group were reemployed in two months compared to the control group. In addition, at the two-month measurement, the guided imagery group felt significantly more control over the job loss than the control group.[1]

---

[1] Joseph, L.M. and Greenberg, M.A. (2001).The effects of a career transition program on reemployment success in laid-off professionals. Journal of Consulting Psychology, vol. 53 (3) pp. 169-181

The unconscious mind works with pictures and metaphors. When we picture in our mind what we want, while also bringing in many of the five senses such as sight, hearing, taste, smell, touch, to couple with our heartfelt emotions and our desire, we create a total mind-body experience of having that which we desire. We are sending out an energetic signal to the Universe and creating a new possibility for ourselves by enlisting the unconscious mind to ally with our conscious mind and our heart's desires. The unconscious mind doesn't know the difference between something that you have done over and over again by visualization with your thoughts, especially when emotions and five senses are integrated into the experience, versus something that you have actually experienced physically. Visualization creates new neurological pathways (possibilities) in the brain, and when you actually go to perform the action, the brain already has the pathway and recognizes the experience as something it has already done time and time again, even though you may have only envisioned it with guided imagery. It's like when the coach calls a play in a basketball game; all the players on the court understand what to do, and where they need to go in order to score a basket, because they've done it in practice a hundred times (if the coach is worth his salt). They know they all have a role on the team, and they all have to take that action in order to score the points. It's like a well-oiled machine. When you visualize what you want, calling in all the emotions, senses, and imagery into a scenario, it's as if you are calling all the players on the court into action in a concerted team effort, working as a unified, group versus your emotions, senses, unconscious and conscious mind working in what could be perceived as unfocused effort.

The Blue Angels put on extraordinary flying shows for the public and they use visualization and verbally rehearse from start to finish before each and every practice and live show. The stakes are high if there is even one small error, so practicing is critical to the success of the team flying in those perfect formations. They verbally and visually go through the preflight checks, getting into the jet, communicating with each pilot (exactly how they will communicate the day of the air show), and going through who will say what and when. They synchronize each and every action and movement that will be made and they practice visually and verbally over and over again, using every detail and sense that they can bring into the practice.

An even earlier pioneer of visualization and imagery work, Dr. B. Naperstek says, "Guided imagery is a directed, deliberate kind of daydream that mobilizes your unconscious to assist with conscious goals." As noted on her Healing Journeys website, Dr. Naperstek's work has been recognized and noted by *Prevention Magazine,* which credited her with "quietly creating an underground revolution among mainstream health and mental health bureaucracies, by persuading major institutions such as the U.S. Veteran's Administration, the U.S. Department of Defense, Kaiser Permanente, Blue Shield of California, United Health Care, Oxford Health Plan, scores of pharmas and nearly 2,000 hospitals and recovery centers to distribute her guided imagery recordings, in many instances free of charge to recipients."

The magazine also noted that she developed "military-friendly resources" with the help of the U.S. Army and the Ft. Sill Resiliency Center, and DCoE (Defense Centers of Excellence), which declared guided imagery one of their Twelve Promising Practices. Dr. Naperstek's audio programs have been involved in over two dozen clinical trials, with nearly a dozen studies completed to date. *Prevention Magazine* noted: "Efficacy has been established for several psychological and medical challenges, most recently for military sexual trauma and combat stress at Duke University Medical Center/Durham Veterans Administration Hospital." [2]

Using visualization is simple and effective, and I believe that its effectiveness is often dismissed because it's so simple to do. People don't think working through difficult situations can possibly be that easy. Visualization is simply a way to tune into a frequency that broadcasts what it is you want to achieve. The idea of mind over matter is the same. You're just lining up the electrons in a way that you would like the outcome to be, or the way you see it as being, regardless of how the reality or situation currently looks.

We all use mind over matter on a daily basis. Our emotions, beliefs and thoughts are reflected back to us, through the way we are experiencing the reality of our life. We are all living out the experience of our life consciously and partway unconsciously, and the way we take that journey, or experience the path and that reality is completely within our ability to create and design. The way we choose to perceive the experience of life is totally

[2] Bellruth Naparstek, LISW, BCD | Health Journeys http://www.healthjourneys.com/Main/Home/Belleruth_Naparstek

up to us. Some people understand this intuitively, and some people take a lifetime to discover the possibilities. When life is unhappy for us, sometimes it's as simple as reaching up and grabbing a new visual script. This can also be described as creating interoperability between your way and life's way. You are pulling in new possibilities and making a pathway for positive changes to happen in your favor. We are all alchemists, essentially learning to use mind over matter.

I know what you could be thinking: What about the placebo effect? How do you know if this is really working or if you are just wanting and believing it to be working? In the beginning, I thought the same thing, which led me to research more about the placebo effect and the part it played into people's ability to achieve outcomes in healing. The placebo effect, according to the Oxford Dictionaries[3], "Is a beneficial effect, produced by a placebo drug or treatment, which cannot be attributed to the properties of the placebo itself, and must therefore be due to the patient's belief in that treatment." If you have a desired outcome actually unfold the way you wanted and believed it should, doesn't it mean that it—whatever it was, the thought, belief, or the pill—must have worked? Regardless, if you think that your mind just made it happen, it happened, did it not? So what if it was your thoughts and beliefs that make it happen? Isn't that the point? Your thoughts (energy) and beliefs (more energy) created the space that provides the outcome you believed to be a possible outcome in the first place. I've had clients come to me for energy healing treatments say, "I

[3] http://www.oxforddictionaries.com/us/definition/american_english/placebo-effect

feel much better; my illness is gone. But how do I know that I didn't just believe it or want it to reverse my problem?" Of course you believed it! That, for sure, was first part of the process of your healing, how else would it happen? There was a belief on some level, whether it was conscious or unconscious. Your thoughts are energy that affects your body (matter) and state of health (also matter).

This takes me down another avenue of thinking; if the validity and power of thoughts and beliefs have so much effect on the body that there is medically recognized terminology for it, then what else could be affected by thoughts and beliefs? How could this apply to other areas in life that need healing, beyond our personal health and wellness? What if we spent more time curating our thoughts, questioning our beliefs, and being a bit more conscious and aware with our habits and actions in our society? Could it be possible to notice a shift for the better?

CHAPTER 3

Carolina On My Mind

"Whether you think you can or you think you can't, you are right."

— Henry Ford

After completing basic training and my military occupation specialty training at the communications school in Augusta, Georgia, my duty station was Fort Bragg, North Carolina, just a few hours' drive from my daughter who was in Virginia with her father. I was able to spend time with her on long weekends and holidays with a driving pass approved by my supervisor. It was still a difficult transition for me, not seeing her more, but with Army life and no support system around me, I was hesitant to bring her back into my life full-time. She would have to be uprooted and have to adjust again. She had just started school and her grandmother drove the school bus that picked her up and dropped her off every day. She was always with family, not with strangers in daycare. She had a great support system and needed that consistency and stability. At that time, staying with her father was still the best situation for her as I was continuing to adapt and transition into the Army and I wouldn't be able to create a stable home for her while also managing to be a soldier.

While checking into my first unit, an aviation unit, I was informed that in eight to ten months, we would be deployed to Bosnia for a year. Things got very busy as we prepared for that deployment. Even though I was just beginning to settle into the military lifestyle, I was excited about the prospect of being deployed to someplace new. Each day we went through new training, either preparing for field exercises or servicing our communications equipment.

Despite my excitement, there was something unsettling, a discord so to speak. I joined the Army partly to improve my situation and better myself, but there was also the part of me that was searching to fit somewhere; an idea that I wanted to belong to something bigger than myself. It became clear after a period of time that the military didn't fit well for me either, and I had a hard time not challenging people that were charged with making the decisions. I didn't get into trouble, but I didn't make my life easier, either. The military fed the conservative side of me and kept me tethered to a safe and secure career path, but there was another aspect of myself that still felt lost; a part that never seemed to click in anywhere. That part kept me curiously seeking to uncover more about the mysterious aspects of myself that weren't being appeased.

Having joined the Army with a little more maturity than the 19-year-old corporal I worked for, there was difficulty watching him fumble around trying to figure out what to do next. On top of that, I was growing irritated living with the daily nonsense of being a private. My sense was that there was still more for me to do than blindly follow and perform menial tasks. We all have to start somewhere though, and being a private was my entry point. Once again, I had to suck it up and make peace with being there. I consoled myself with the acknowledgement that this was leading me down the road to something greater. By no means was this going to be it. At that point in my life as a private, no one could have begun to explain to me that it would be the route that led me to land where I am today. It supports the idea that progress, however we define it, comes from beginning somewhere, regardless of what we think we know about the path ahead or even how we see our life unfolding. Anywhere on that path is just fine. We just have to be willing to take some steps and begin.

Although there was a vision or broad view of my future possibilities, I knew experience and more education was needed. If I dwelled on these obstacles for too long, it would be discouraging. Even so, there was frustration within me that more of my future path couldn't be seen, and life still felt jumbled and unsettled for me. The way I envisioned myself still wasn't matching up with where I actually stood; nothing seemed to happen fast enough for me. As a way to bridge the gap, I began taking classes in the information technology field at the local community college. During this time, the Army tuition assistance plan paid for 75 percent of college tuition for active duty soldiers. It was unbelievable to me that anyone would pay that much for me to go to college, so I took advantage of it.

On another front, I was disappointed. The incoming Bush Administration halted all the deployments preparing to leave for Bosnia. Many members of my unit had worked for months to prepare for our peacekeeping presence there. Although excitement had built up and I was looking forward to the adventure, part of me was relieved not to be leaving the country, so far away from Jordan. Communication would have been a bit more complicated from overseas since technology wasn't what it is today. My daughter was still pretty little and talking on the phone with her often lasted two to four minutes before she dropped the phone and was on to something else. Although it was difficult for me to connect with her in those years I did see her on weekend trips, driving there as often as possible.

While establishing myself at my new duty station, which would be home for a few years, I got used to the life rhythm of being a soldier. There was ease in making new friends and I even found myself adopting a few new family members. Oftentimes, the people I worked with got together on the weekends at each other's homes for barbeques or for nights out. There was a real camaraderie amongst our platoon members, and certainly a sense of deep loyalty to each other. In a way, it felt that because we were all away from where we came from, we were all watching out for each other, like family would.

After spending a couple of years in the Army, living in Fayetteville, North Carolina, I met someone. We were both active duty and stationed at Fort Bragg. We dated for a little over a year and then got engaged. We had a great time together in the beginning; he was exciting, smart and a Green Beret. I admired his strength and at the same time his aloofness about life. He didn't take himself too seriously; in fact, he didn't take much of anything too seriously. From my perspective, everything was pretty serious; I was still figuring out how to step beyond just survival. He made me laugh a lot, teased me when I was too hard or stern with myself.

Shortly after 9/11, deployments to Afghanistan were starting to ramp up. In the planning of our future, we decided I should be the one to get out of the Army because it became apparent with the direction things were going, we would never see each other if one of us didn't stay home. His group would most definitely play a large role in the efforts that would take place in Afghanistan, and he was further along in his career, and higher in rank. He also had a much cooler job, and I envied his adventures. I had enough training in communications at that point and had been working on college credits and training certification credentials while learning as much as possible through on-the-job training in the Army. Getting out was a no brainer since I had a job easily lined up for me, doing the same thing but making nearly three times the pay. I checked out of the Army on Friday and started my new job the following Monday.

A few months later, my fiancé found out that he was deploying just as we were in the final process of purchasing a house. We knew we would have just enough time to close and move in before he would be shipped off to Afghanistan. He woke up one morning, rolled over, and declared, "It's Tuesday, we should get married." I said, "What's Tuesday got to do with anything?" "It's as good of a day as any," he told me. "We were planning to get married anyway. We might as well do it now. We'll have a real wedding and tell our family later." He was a pretty spontaneous guy; admittedly that part of him was exciting to me. After calling in sick to work, we went down to the courthouse and, on a Tuesday morning, we got hitched. A sweet North Carolina couple in their 70's served as our witnesses. We didn't tell many people, only a couple of close friends and a few close family members. Since it was his first marriage, he wanted an actual wedding so that his family could be a part of it. For me, the thought of sending out a second set of wedding invitations was uncomfortable. Even so, we planned to have a proper wedding and a honeymoon after he returned home from his deployment.

The day after we closed on the house, all of our household goods were finally moved in, and he left for six months in Afghanistan. I was neck deep in boxes and had a jigsaw of furniture in each room. Night after night and on the weekends, I worked through getting our house set up and in order. My mother and daughter came for the summer and helped me put things together, as well as helped me plan the wedding, which was scheduled for a month after he returned from the deployment. We wrote a lot of letters back and forth, and once every few weeks I would get an email from him. He was pretty busy, and the connectivity and access to email was limited. We both worked very hard to stay connected with frequent letters throughout the deployment and soon enough he was back home, and we were finalizing our wedding plans.

We had a small, but nice wedding and everything went beautifully. My mother was there and my daughter was the flower girl. We had a great celebration, followed by a fun and memorable honeymoon in the Caribbean before coming back to our normal lives. Soon after returning, we got word he would be heading out for another deployment just a few months after Christmas. It wasn't happy news; we were just starting to get settled in as a married couple. Still, there wasn't much room to complain. That was what I had signed up for, being married to a soldier instead of being the soldier.

Getting married seemed like a good idea and the next step for us. Logically speaking, it was. Everything made sense on paper. With the deployment schedule, we ended up spending more time apart than together as a married couple and this took a toll on us both. Emotionally, when we were together, it started to look like the home volcano science experiment of mixing baking soda and vinegar together and watching the explosive mess spill out all over the kitchen floor. As months went by, and from one deployment to the next, the relationship became even more volatile. There hadn't been enough time for us to bond or establish our relationship's foundation. Tensions mounted as our pre-marriage emotional baggage and unresolved issues began showing up. There were good days and then there were some really bad days. No amount of marriage counseling could recover what we had lost. He would come home still amped up from the last deployment, looking for a fight. I had spent a good part of my own life always fighting for something. Fighting to survive, fighting to make it through something hard, and fighting to prove myself professionally. There was no fight left in me for a relationship that had gone from intoxicating to toxic. We both questioned the value of what we were fighting for within the marriage.

I was unhappy, and each day was filled with growing disappointment within myself for what I had yet to achieve.

Being there, at home, waiting for him, made me feel trapped and confined. This discontent coupled with his emotional state coming back from one combat deployment after another. Essentially, it was the perfect storm. We were both still trying to deal with our emotional discord, very adamant and selfish about what we thought we each deserved. Neither of us would wave the white flag and put the other's needs before our own. We both lacked the commitment to work through the hard things with each other's best interest in mind.

The marriage had its purpose and values, letting me know what I didn't want my life to be, especially at that time. No matter how hard I tried for married life to be right for me, my life couldn't be that. I had thought getting married would make me whole, giving me a place to fit in with someone while continuing to figure out my life. After getting married and leaving the Army, my feelings of being lost were compounded and left me desiring a tribe to belong to. Regardless of my efforts, emotionally I still did not feel like my life was "together."

This marriage was my second, so there shouldn't have been surprises about what I was getting into. Once again, I hadn't correctly assessed the level of commitment required. I was nowhere near ready or prepared to give that level of selfless commitment and support to someone else. It sounds selfish, but it's the simple truth. Getting married to a soldier meant sacrificing myself and putting my career on hold in order to support him in his because we were stationed in North Carolina for the long haul. For my career, it felt like I had just laced up my running shoes, barely put my feet in the starting blocks, and then someone called off the race.

It wasn't like I could just get up and move to the next great opportunity career-wise. For years, I would be limited to the geographic location of where he was stationed. Each time he came home, we were more distant and removed from each other. When we tried to do things together, we would inevitably argue. He saw me growing more and more dissatisfied, depressed, tired, and impatient, working in what I characterized as the most boring computer help desk job on the planet, ever. The same feelings I had when I was getting ready to join the Army and leave my small town were beginning to bubble to the surface again. That feeling inside of me was back and it said, "This isn't it, you need to keep going."

As the joy and novelty of marriage wore off, the idea of another divorce began to sink in. The longer he stayed away for his job, the more apparent this reality was becoming to me. I realized how unfair this was for him, because my decision and emotional closure all played out when he was deployed. For him, while deployed, our life hit the pause button, and he was focused on trying to keep himself and his team alive in the midst of a major conflict in Afghanistan. I still supported him as much as possible while he was there. Doing fundraisers and attending events with the other wives, my mind stayed busy and allowed me to work through things slowly without too much solitude to obsess over every detail. Nonetheless, my emotions were processing around the reality of failed marriage *numero duo*. I felt deep guilt for taking him down the road of being together forever before realizing it wasn't really possible for me. I wasn't in it for better or worse. When things got worse, I wasn't willing to put up with the situation. Also we both struggled with the person he became each time he came home.

Wars do change people, but perhaps each time he came home, I became someone else too. Everything felt like a mismatch, even having him in my bed felt like I was sleeping next to a stranger. We were both uncomfortable, and he tried to overcompensate by being overly doting and affectionate. This, of course, only made things worse, especially since emotionally I had already begun to feel disconnected from him. There was a deep process of introspection and questioning as to why I couldn't just be one of those women who got married and lived happily ever after at home, supporting her husband. Fears resurfaced. Sitting alone, I repeatedly asked myself, "Can I do this again; step into the world alone?" The answer was consistent, "You're never really alone."

My mind was made up that when he returned from the fourth deployment, I would ask him for a divorce. Time was up for sacrificing one more day, not doing the things that I felt happy and passionate about. I knew if I stayed with him there would always be a piece of me that felt resentful that he was able to do what he wanted in his career, while I was expected to sit at home and follow him. I would never really be happy or be able to make peace with that situation.

I believed that being married would fulfill that missing piece or yearning deep inside me for something more, a place to be. But it didn't, not at all. In some ways, it made it worse because being married meant being more settled and more settled is the opposite of what I needed in my life at that time, especially since I was also yearning for fulfillment through experiencing, which I believed would come through more professional achievements. There was something I was looking for in my dreams of having adventures. Sitting at home doing the daily grind, with our relationship on hold, while he was having the dynamic career, living out his passion, and having great and memorable adventures did not appeal to me. Part of me felt a need for the security he provided to me financially. In the past I was in the habit of struggling financially and still hadn't fully come into or realized my own strength and independence. I wrestled back and forth with this desire to take a leap into something new and amazing again, leaving what was known and comfortable.

The vivid dreams started showing up again, as they do whenever I'm working through emotional aspects of life transitions. Dreams of traveling, working and living in the Middle East were starting to come through. In those dreams, there was never anyone standing beside me. I was alone, as I had always been, in all my visions throughout my journey. Having those dreams and visions made me more conscious of a theme in my life; I'm always alone, doing whatever it is that needs to get done by myself. It felt like no one would ever really be there to back me up, pick me up or support me if I fell during the really big things in my life. Friends supported me to an extent, but there are limits to what can be asked of friends and then there are my own personal responsibilities, and accountability for choices that are made. It isn't that there aren't people in my life; there have always been people, lots of people. I know my family cares about me, that isn't the point. The fact is everything that had been achieved and accomplished in my life was done through my own efforts. Life, for me, was an exercise in proving I could count on myself and that no matter what happened, I was going to be okay.

I found myself questioning my deepest desires. What's a "normal life," and why wasn't that enough for me? The thought of the traditional "Leave It to Beaver" life bored me to tears. I wanted to have exciting experiences, learn more about other ways of living, and understand how things worked in different parts of the world. I wanted to meet new people and see things from a different perspective. I was sick of hearing about other people's adventures, especially my husband's, seeing the pictures and hearing all the stories. I wanted those experiences for myself.

During my time as a military wife, I met a small group of like-minded ladies within a spiritually minded community. The Open Door was a group of mostly women; some were military wives whose husbands were deployed often and in the same unit as my husband. We spent a lot of time together while our husbands were away. Most of the ladies of the Open Door found a common interest for healthy living and well-being through books and various community classes like yoga, cooking, meditation, energy healing, massage, dream circles, and other classes. I did my first yoga class at the Open Door and got my first real exposure to the application of energy healing modalities. I became certified and started working with a few people. There were some interesting healing results and slowly my interests expanded to learn about other types of alternative healing methods. Nothing really stuck with me enough to prompt me to quit my job and pursue healing full-time. But I had this sense that the body was capable of healing itself, given the right conditions with these methods.

The community of women at the Open Door was a supportive and safe community. This allowed me to explore a new and expanded perspective of life and myself. The support of that community gave me the space to work through and make sense of what I was experiencing and going through with myself and with my husband.

The community that was built there at that time fostered lifelong friendships and learning, opened the door for so many new possibilities, and connected people in the community in so many different ways. I don't think Susan and Jennifer, my lifelong friends and soul sisters, realized then the impact that the Open Door would have on all of our lives and on the community. We didn't know we were making lifelong friendships and bonds. Today, I can call either one of those ladies and no matter how long it's been or where I am in the world, our conversation will pick up where it left off as if no time has passed. The Open Door was ahead of its time in so many ways. It was perfect for what our little community of wives needed during difficult times, adjustments, and healing to the 15-year long cycle of war and deployments. Grass roots organizations like these help people and communities, hold things together, and build strong support systems. It's a place of collaboration to provide a better way for people to cope at the most basic human level. It's an outlet and avenue for creating extended family when most military families are living far away from their hometowns. The Open Door was a unique tribe where everyone found an aspect of himself or herself to fit in. I can't imagine how my journey would have unfolded without their support and encouragement. It became the support system that gave me the courage to leap forward to new adventures.

Soon after my husband returned from the deployment to Afghanistan, sapped and unable to find middle ground in the relationship, we reached a tipping point of irreconcilable differences and, as planned, I asked for a divorce. It wasn't easy for either one of us. He was angry and felt powerless to otherwise influence my decision. I was frustrated and felt guilty leaving him behind. We were both emotionally exhausted from the constant confrontation and were ready to end the cycling of emotional turmoil. For the most part, I had already processed the idea of divorce during the last six months that he was gone. I was ready to move on. It got mean and ugly between us for a period of time, which I regretted. We both lacked the maturity to behave well enough and decently to each other. He wanted to try and I wasn't willing to negotiate staying together five minutes longer than needed. There was a lot of blame in both directions. Today, I would have been stronger and willing to share responsibility for the circumstances of our marriage and the ending of things. I still have memories of the excitement and joy he brought to my daughter's life and my life. He was a critical part of my personal evolution. Without those difficult times, the deep introspection wouldn't have been possible. Without the emotional triggers being pulled to the surface through our relationship troubles, the personal healing and resolution done at that time maybe wouldn't have occurred. There were a lot of lessons that came out of that relationship for both of us. One, for sure, was that we both needed to have the freedom to be who we were while still being together. That was where it all fell apart. We were looking for what we expected each other to be, rather than accepting each other as we were and finding a way to make the journey work. Several years later, we made amends over the things that happened. I believe we are both better for having known each other during that period of time.

Having made peace with the situation, I now think he is a fine soul, who has made a lot of effort and progress to heal and better himself. I have respect for people who can transform themselves. It can be hard to admit flaws and faults, and at the same time hold on to self-worth. Being able to hold to a higher standard, while taking action to change into a better version, takes courage. Time and again, the parts that we want to leave behind are often stubborn reminders of who we used to be. Those aspects rear up in the healing process and can be hard to let go. As the well-known inspirational author Bob Proctor says, "This life isn't for lightweights."

CHAPTER 4

Kuwait or Bust

"Not all those who wander are lost."

—J.R.R. Tolkien

Once the decision was made to move on from my second marriage, the Universe cooperated, and the stars aligned (as they do). Within two weeks, I had a job offer in hand for a contract position supporting the Army in Information Technology operations as an Information Systems Security Officer on Camp Doha, Kuwait, and the reporting date, was in three weeks. My house was on the market for less than a day. We received an acceptable offer, and it sold; the whole process went quickly and seamlessly.

The transition began by moving some things into storage, giving things away to charity, while also packing items to move across the world. I still have no idea how things all fell into place so quickly. Through the process, my dear friends from The Open Door, Jenn and her husband Rob, let me stay at their house. They were instrumental in helping me move through this major transition to the next phase of my life. In my opinion, Jenn and Rob are real live human incarnations of earth angels. I'm so thankful for all they did to support me. I was an emotional basket case, trying to handle my move while also dealing with the end of my marriage. There were items left in my house after the closing. They moved those things out and did the cleaning that needed to be done before turning the keys over to the real estate agent. My car was left behind, as well as many personal items, large furniture, and appliances. My mail was being forwarded to their house; bills were coming in from all directions. Jenn, who was taking care of her children and dealing with her husband being deployed, stepped in to manage the pieces of my life that lingered behind and juggled it all perfectly. I could not have done it without her.

When the big news was broken to my family back home, they were less than impressed with my latest job opportunity. There were questions about how this would work with my daughter and whether I would be safe in Kuwait. My arrival to Kuwait would only be a little more than a year after the initial "shock and awe" in Iraq that started in 2003. More troops were piling into Iraq by the day, and the embedded journalists were reporting the news live, showing play-by-plays of the war. I would be living and working only a few hours south by car of where all this activity was taking place.

My plan was to come home for the holidays and summers to spend time with my daughter. In between, however, it was hard to imagine how we would remain in contact. The opportunity seemed like a good thing for my career, and financially it would give me the boost needed to cut the debt noose from around my neck once and for all. I knew it was a risky way to get ahead though, and my time with my daughter was going to be sacrificed. With the distance and time zone it would be difficult to be as active in her life. At the time, I was driven by a sense of achieving more professionally so a better financial future and quality of life could be created for us both.

My family's concern for my safety was justified since American contractors were getting their heads chopped off by extremists. Family members were also a bit perplexed as to what happened with my marriage; they didn't completely understand the ending or my reasoning for walking away. There were a lot of questions from friends and family alike wondering what kind of life I was planning on having in a region of the world that oppressed and treated women poorly. Many asked, "how could you be happy there if you thought being married was so repressive?" Of course there were no real answers because I didn't know what I was walking into. Maybe I was naive, but the unknown factor didn't bother me as much as the feeling of sitting at home in bondage for so long did. I wanted a new adventure. The idea of being in a new place really excited me, even if that new place was the Middle East during a major crisis. I knew that my opportunities for traveling were just beginning and that there was more for me to do, see, and experience. Intuitively, I sensed that, as before, things would work out.

My new employer notified me that along with the company's other employees, I would be living in an apartment building in the city of Salmiya. Living in the city would be exciting and certainly more appealing than living on an Army base. Yet, I was concerned that having all the employees living in one building would provide an easy target for extremists. Company officials reassured me that the building had security around the clock and was considered safe. I did additional research online and also spoke to people already living there. Most of them told me they had only experienced a peaceful coexistence with the locals while living in Kuwait.

Kuwait had gone through a turbulent and violent time. In 1990, Saddam Hussein invaded Kuwait in the middle of the night. Within hours the Kuwaiti troops were defeated, and the Emir, his family, and other government leaders fled to Saudi Arabia. The United Nations Security Council condemned the hostile takeover and initiated a worldwide trade ban. Of particular concern was that Iraq gained about 20 percent of the world's oil reserves as a result of the invasion. There was also concern that Saddam was not finished and might go further south. Shortly after the trade ban, American troops started to deploy to Saudi Arabia and Operation Desert Shield began forming. Over 700,000 troops, including 32 international allies, took part in the U.S.-operation. The UN Council issued an ultimatum with a deadline to the Iraqi president, stating he had until January 16, 1991 to leave Kuwait (a country he was now boldly declaring to be a province of Iraq), or he would be removed by force. The deadline came and went, and the operation went into full effect. On February 24, 1991, after six weeks of air strikes, the ground war began and lasted about four days.[4] Unlike what Saddam had portrayed, the Iraqi troops were ill equipped to defend their position. At

---

[4] http://www.history.com/this-day-in-history/iraq-invades-kuwait

that point, the Iraqi troops, looking more like sacrificial lambs, surrendered, retreated, or got killed in the military operation. My brother, an active duty Marine at the time, deployed and supported Operation Desert Shield with Task Force Ripper. He told stories when he returned about how Marines had encountered hundreds of Iraqis surrendering, terrified and starving to death in the desert. Those Iraqi soldiers had to be desperate if they felt safer in the hands of U.S. Marines rather than retreating or fighting it out in the desert.

Once the ceasefire was declared by President George H. W. Bush and Kuwait was liberated, the country declared a national holiday, Kuwait Liberation Day, celebrated on the 24th and 25th of February. This day is still widely celebrated in Kuwait today with public gatherings and parades organized by various civic groups and part of the government.

One year I took part in the Kuwait Liberation Day celebration with friends. Doing so led to some realizations and discoveries about myself and other expats, not to mention that it was a really good time. There were fireworks; everyone was out enjoying the city and watching the impressive displays in the sky. The younger generation introduced us to the "foam wars," in which basically everyone was spraying each other with canisters of water-based foam. Sitting in a café, it can be shocking to be an unsuspecting recipient of the foam spray by locals. One year, eager to not miss the good fun, my roommate and I decided, if you can't beat 'em, join 'em. Filling our backpacks with the foam canisters, we hit the streets and recruited some smaller Kuwaiti children to our team. We were covered from head to toe in foam at the end and had a great time. Not all Americans we worked with were so open to participating in the celebrations, and often complained about the inconvenience of the culture and the festivities. That attitude could be comparable to how some foreigners that come to our country react to American customs and culture and are sometimes unwilling to leave their small communities or are wary of integrating and speaking the language. Cultural separation and divides exist on both sides of the equation, no matter what country you are from. To me, it seems like the best way to experience what a culture is really all about is to fully jump in and embrace it.

After Operation Desert Shield, Kuwait and the United States developed an allied relationship. We had two contingency bases, several small forward operating bases (FOBs) run by the Army, and an airbase, run by the U.S. Air Force. It was hard for me to imagine that there would be much animosity toward me, an American living in Kuwait. However, foreign politics operate at a different, higher level than the feeling and sentiments of the everyday people I would meet. Nevertheless, I reasoned, if stuff hit the fan, there were places for me to go.

After the conflict was resolved, Kuwait became pretty westernized. There were McDonald's, Wendy's, Subway's, Ruby Tuesday's, TGI Friday's, Applebee's and magnificent shopping malls with all the name brands familiar to Americans. For goodness sakes, I thought. It couldn't be that terrible. In the early 2000s, there was little information on the Internet about Kuwait. Measuring 6,880 square miles, it's a very small country only a little bigger than Connecticut, and the population at that time was about three million people.[5] The primary language is Arabic, but English was widely spoken by almost everyone. Islam makes up 85 percent of the religious practice; however, a few other religions are practiced as well, and Kuwait City has a Christian church for Christian worshippers. I was surprised to learn that there was an active Christian church, and as a westerner, it strengthened my resolve that it was probably peaceful enough for me to live there. Luckily, I knew a few people working there for the Army and living in the surrounding cities. They assured me it was pretty quiet and safe for westerners. I was excited and despite some lingering apprehension, as well as continuing disapproval from family and friends, I believed it would be okay to take this leap.

It felt good to shed most of my personal belongings before leaving. It was symbolic of letting go of my old life, purging what was no longer needed or what no longer served me; it was a necessary part of the transitioning and healing process of the life I was leaving behind. It felt critical to do in order to move forward, like I was making room in my life for everything to be new. When the purge was complete, all my worldly possessions easily fit into a small five-by-eight foot storage unit, while two suitcases and a trunk were shipped to Kuwait ahead of me.

Travel day arrived. With $21.23 to my name, my mother loaned me $400 to get me through until my first paycheck. Walking through the gate to board the small puddle jumper sitting on the runway in Fayetteville, North Carolina, I began to realize how much my life was going to change.

---

[5] https://en.wikipedia.org/wiki/Kuwait

Looking up, I saw my mom standing at the window where non-passengers were stopped by security. I could tell she was scared for me as she watched me get on the plane; even though she would never say it, it was all over her face. As hard as the goodbye was for us, I realized that she never once questioned my decisions and always respected my pursuits, no matter how crazy they seemed. She may have been scared—as any parent rightly would be—but she understood and believed in me, long before I believed in myself.

A new perspective was gained that day and something clicked. I realized that it would never really matter who supported or agreed with me, and who didn't. Everyone was always going to have an opinion. When I'm excited about doing anything in life, I run toward it; no one can talk me out of it or convince me otherwise. If it turned into a mess, my strength would carry me through the clean-up process. The sense of needing anyone to accept me, give me permission, or agree with my life was over. When the dust settled, it was only me standing there holding the broom and the dustpan anyway.

I barely made my connecting flight to Amsterdam. This was my first trip across the world. My stress level was still high, post-separation process, selling the house, moving, and packing inside of a couple weeks. Such a whirlwind! With not much time to process, I was walking on eggshells.

The seven-hour flight was crowded and seemed to go on forever. Thanks to a screaming child who kicked the back of my seat the entire flight, it was impossible to get any rest. Arriving in Amsterdam, I was excited to see a new place, even if it was just an airport. Things looked very contemporary and bright and there were people from every culture moving in every direction, briskly pulling luggage behind them. Wading through the waves of human traffic, I found my next gate. There was four hours to wait before my flight to Kuwait City. A couple of contractors decided to leave the airport to visit an Amsterdam coffee shop where marijuana was readily available. "You wanna come with us?" One guy asked me. "No thanks," I told him. "I don't smoke and I'd be a nervous wreck about getting back in time." "You don't know what you're missing." Feeling annoyed by his persistence, I replied, "Knock yourself out buddy. Uncle Sam and Mary Jane aren't friends in my world." Those working for the government are frequently tested for drug use and there was no way I would do anything to risk my job, nor was I going to risk having an issue with Dutch customs officials and possibly miss my flight. Those types of risks were not at all appealing to me.

Waiting for my flight gave me plenty of time to think. While I was excited, I was also anxious. My expectations about my future life in Kuwait were all over the place. What if people were right? Was I nuts to go to this extreme to get a high-paying job? I was moving to a country where my American freedoms wouldn't count for much. I recognized the irony of starting my life over and getting away from my own situation that felt like bondage, by going to a part of the world where women were essentially in bondage. With every big transition in my life, there have always been lingering feelings of doubt, because I can't see the outcome until the dust has nearly settled. Looking at my options, other career prospects, my bills weren't going to pay themselves, and there were a lot of bills. Besides, a good adventure was what I had been dreaming of, despite my doubts. The fear of the unknown was a little exciting to me.

Glancing around the gate's waiting area, everyone looked exhausted. I propped my feet on top of my suitcase, laid my head back, and slept for the remaining three hours. When we finally boarded the plane, I felt like a zombie, barely able to shuffle my feet forward. Since the flight was mostly empty, I was able to stretch out across a few seats and get a few more hours of sleep.

I woke up as we made our descent into Kuwait City. I could see the city lights and some large buildings. The street below looked as busy as any in a major city. So far nothing looked much different. A family was sitting a few rows in front of me. The woman was wearing a *hijab*, the traditional head covering worn by some Muslim women in Kuwait and other Gulf countries. These days we've all become accustomed to seeing women donning the *hijab*. That was my first exposure, however, to seeing this symbol of modesty and privacy. Despite my mother's admonitions about not staring running through my head, I was curious. After a few moments, I managed to turn my attention back out the window. Just as the wheels touched the runway, passengers on the plane started clapping. That's concerning, I thought. Was there ever a question that we wouldn't be landing?

Stepping off of the plane and standing in the makings of what looked like it could be a line to get a visa, the madness began. I really came to appreciate the bureaucracy of the United States. Though we have our share of problems, we are pretty organized. Our immigration and customs process, for the most part, is an ordered, well-oiled machine.

Not so in the Kuwait International Airport, where I found myself engulfed in a sea of people pushing from every direction. Another flight carrying dozens of migrant workers from other parts of Asia had arrived nearly at the same time as ours. Standing at five-feet, eight-inches, I towered over them by at least six to eight inches, and probably outweighed them all by fifty pounds or more. There was no order or formal line anywhere; people were just shoving their way through, making the scene chaotic, confusing, and a little frightening. There was no polite way to go about this; I was going to have to use my size to get through the line. When in Rome, do as the Romans. After a few feet of forward movement, the sea of people began to part and I found myself practically at the front of the quasi visa line. The man behind the counter smiled at me and took my money in exchange for the visa. Visa in hand, I headed to a more orderly line to have my passport stamped and was finally off to gather my luggage at the baggage claim. Since Kuwait is a dry country in which alcohol was banned, my bags were passed through a security screening set up to prevent alcohol and other forbidden items from being brought into the country. While the security laws seemed strict, I witnessed people who were leaving Kuwait carelessly waved through security checkpoints, even though the metal detectors were clearly going off. Months after, I learned that the guards often seized illegal alcohol, only to turn around and sell it on the black market at three or four times the original cost. Or you could even be invited to an underground party where everyone there happened to be drinking what they took from you earlier. It was also quite strange to me that there was more security screening of passengers entering the country, than there were of those leaving the country. At that time, they didn't have the serious TSA pre-flight screening that US and European passengers did before flying.

At any rate, as we finished the security inspection, the big metal doors opened, and we walked down a center aisle. The sides of the aisle were lined shoulder to shoulder with people. There were men dressed in *dishdashas*, or the traditional long-sleeved white robes with the red and white-checkered headdress. Women were wearing *hijabs* and *abayas*, or black, full-body dresses. In addition to the *abaya*, many were also wearing the *niqab*, which totally covered their mouths and noses, leaving just their eyes exposed. Some of the westerners and Kuwaitis referred to them as "ninjas." The culture shock was setting in. While everyone around me seemed covered up, I felt naked walking those thirty feet to the curb, pulling my luggage behind me. A man was holding up a sign with my last name scribbled in black magic marker. People were still moving in every direction, cutting me off with massive luggage carts. Though it was midnight, it was the busiest airport I had ever seen. There were small Indian boys in blue uniforms pushing large carts stacked with luggage. There were people hugging and reuniting with their families, walking slowly and talking. My associate weaved through the crowd like an expert, meeting me half way. He quickly introduced himself and explained that we needed to walk to pick up the car in the garage, and that it wouldn't be that much farther.

After a long ride in the dark, with me being almost too exhausted to keep up with the conversation, we eventually got to the company apartment. I couldn't wait to lay my head down for a nice long sleep. Pushing open the tall wooden door, my colleague helped carry in my luggage, dropped it on the floor, told me that he'd be back in the morning, and said goodbye. After locking the door behind him, I stood for a moment taking it all in. The sterile living room, with white walls and basic furniture, smelled like new construction and dust. The walls were cement and the floors marble. The couch, chair, and curtains were an unappealing green.

The kitchen boasted blue tile and all the necessary equipment. Even though I'm not much of a homemaker, it was nice to recognize a stove, refrigerator, and microwave. The apartment was large, with three bedrooms. I chose the one in the far corner of the apartment, far away from the busy street below with constant traffic and endless honking.

Mailing some things to myself in Kuwait weeks before allowed me to travel light. I had packed my sheets, pillow, and a small blanket, thinking that having them would help me sleep in comfort in the new surroundings. For some reason, something as small as having my pillow made me feel a bit more at ease.

After taking a shower, I crawled into my newly made bed and turned off the light. Despite feeling exhausted, I remained wide awake and my mind was racing. For the first time in my life, there was no calling 911 if there was an emergency. If someone broke in, what would I do? There was a rotary phone in the apartment, but whom would I even call? I kept thinking about all the things that could happen and how I could end up as another Westerner statistic in the Middle East on the evening news. My family was right; I might be nuts. Was it really necessary for me to come here? What always drove me to leave home, where safety was assured and there were few unknowns? Not considering myself a religious woman, not even considering myself to be Catholic any more, I prayed to God that night. I also prayed to every saint and angel that came to mind, hoping they would surround me and protect me in my new surroundings. Finally, I fell asleep.

Hours later, I was woken with the sounds of a man yelling in Arabic. I didn't know whether we were under attack or just being scolded. After so many minutes the man's voice stopped. It was a less than ideal way to learn that my apartment was next door to a large prayer mosque. Looking at my watch, I saw that it was just past five a.m. Most practicing Muslims pray five times a day, known as Salat times, and the first call to prayer starts at early dawn, or morning twilight and is called Fajr.

Now wide-awake, I decided to get up and do something productive before starting work. After unpacking and putting my things away, I turned the TV on and was surprised to see several recognizable channels. A music video station played hip-hop music from England, while the U.S. stations had Judge Judy, Oprah, CNN International, TNT, and a few other stations that played familiar shows from home.

It was astonishing to see such a liberal array of channels on regular cable TV, all with Arabic subtitles of course. I watched a report on CNN about fighting going on an hour or so north (by car) in Iraq. People were not just dying, but they were sacrificing themselves for a cause they believed was bigger and more important than themselves.

It made my problems seem small. So in that moment, I made a conscious decision that it was time for me to move past the drama and self-pity that had dominated my perspective regarding my life and two divorces. Tears started rolling down my face. It was the first time I had ever really given myself time or permission to cry over my divorce. The accumulated stress just built up inside of me. Crying allowed me to release all those feelings. The moment was about making peace with my past and ridding myself of the frustrations, doubt, guilt, and stress that had dominated my life.

A new agreement was made to live my life as though it was the great adventure my mind had always seen it to be, and to stay focused on my overall life objectives. There was a drive inside of me to achieve something professionally, to become successful in my own right. Additionally, the paradigm had to be broken to create more options for my daughter than were ever available for me. If it were not I, then who else would set an example for her that women could be strong, independent, and successful without a partner? So far, almost every woman she knew on both sides of her family got pregnant and married very young. This isn't a bad thing, after all it is the path I took, however it can be a difficult and limiting path. I noticed the pattern and it made me concerned for her future. I just wanted to show her other life possibilities, but I also wanted to be able to provide her with rich cultural experiences that might be otherwise impossible with limited finances. This was one of many ideals that reminded me why I set out on this journey in the first place, and I couldn't lose sight of that.

While living in Kuwait, my intention was to experience life with a different set of eyes, eyes that were open and non-judgmental about the culture and the people I was seeing. Being in that part of the world, there were endless opportunities to learn about the culture right in front of me. I wanted to understand more about the religion and the differences between their culture and mine.

On my first day of work, a coworker drove to show two fellow workers and myself the route to work. The drive took about 45 minutes and he drove the car like it was stolen and he was frantic to escape capture. Within 100 meters of leaving our apartment complex, we were injected into a massive traffic circle with speeding cars weaving in and out in no particular order or sequence. All three passengers cringed as we were repeatedly nearly sideswiped or rear-ended. "We call this the circle of death," our driver shouted. "You have to drive hard here or you'll get hit, and it will always be your fault because you're a foreigner." "What do you do if you do get hit?" I asked. He looked at me in his rear view mirror and smiled, "I don't recommend getting hit." That was reassuring. We made it through the first gauntlet to the major motorway. Although we were going pretty fast, cars passed us like we were barely moving. The highways seemed lawless, with drivers driving at top speeds in the far left lane of the highway, much like the Autobahn. Cars would weave across three lanes at a time, cutting off rows of traffic just to make an exit on the far right at the last minute. Other cars were going so fast that they sometimes seemed only a blur.

Since it was daytime, there was more to see. The driver pointed out the American Embassy, which was good to know. The houses looked like they were either stucco or cement made, and ranged from smaller homes, to mini mansions, to even larger, more impressive-looking palaces. Some looked gaudy to me, with gold trimming around the windows and doorways, exotic fixtures, bright colors, and marble pillars. Others were conservative and looked like something you could see in a nicer, higher-end California neighborhood. Most places had tall metal fences and gates around them. Pockets of the city looked like they had been built and specifically designated for communities of apartment buildings. Additionally, there were a number of well-known landmarks that people often asked about, including the massive blue and white water towers that resembled giant, fancy martini glasses.

Finally, we arrived at Camp Doha, where we would be working. Cars were lined-up and making their way through the cement barriers. "It is like this every day?" I asked. "Pretty much, just depends on when you get here. Sometimes it's even more backed up," our driver replied. It was about seven a.m. and it took us 40 minutes to get to the main security checkpoint. How much earlier did we need to leave? Once it was finally our turn for the security check, everyone was instructed to leave their items in the car and open any bags or purses, as well as the doors, trunk, and hood of the vehicle. We all stepped to the side while the guards did the security sweep, went around the bottom of the car with mirrors, and checked all the inside compartments of the car for any bombs or prohibited items. The U.S. Army was very serious about upholding the Kuwaiti laws, and if you were found entering in possession of alcohol, drugs, pornographic material, or unauthorized weapons, you would immediately be barred from base and lose your job.

50 minutes later we arrived at the building on Camp Doha where we would be working. Just getting to work seemed like quite the trek, no telling what the rest of the day had in store. As soon as we were all checked in, I found it a relief to be around Americans, something familiar to me. I wasn't crazy about my job, a basic computer technical job, resetting passwords and enforcing local security policies. However, there was room to grow, as well as plenty of travel ahead and things to do in the city that would keep my mind occupied.

The base was on the smaller side, mostly consisting of buildings that looked like warehouses where active duty military lived while they did their tour in Kuwait. There was a dining facility, gym, and also a basic Post Exchange (PX) for shopping, where you could find the essential hygiene goods, some clothing, DVD's, music, and a limited amount of small electronics. There was also a Starbucks, Subway, some other fast food places, as well as an Internet café. It was nice to recognize some of the American brands, things that could all be bought with U.S. currency. The Kuwaiti Dinar (dollar) was very strong; almost three times the U.S. Dollar. Being able to pick up the basics was a convenient benefit for contractors working on base. Another benefit of working for the military overseas was being able to use the Army Post Office (APO) services. It made ordering anything online or correspondence to and from the family easy, and usually only took about one to two weeks to receive a package, depending on the time of year. The mail was delivered directly to our building, which helped save money on things that didn't have to be bought downtown.

Other than shopping, going to the gym, working and discovering new ways to get the comforts of home to Kuwait there wasn't much else happening on the Army base. Some of my new colleagues liked to talk about the early days when things were a bit wilder. They told me about an American contractor who left work one night, and while sitting at a red light just off base was shot and killed by a gunman hiding in a bush. They told me it was one of the only things that had been alarming for contractors in a while, but that if I was driving alone at night and it was clear, to just go through that light and never stop.

We were introduced to everyone, and I quickly made friends with another American contractor working in the building with us, Tony, a guy in his late 40's. He grew up in New York City and still had a strong New York accent. He told me not to worry, that the city was mostly safe, and I was lucky to have gotten there when I did. He told me about when the chemical threat level was higher and everyone worried about chemical attacks, and the base commander issued an order that all personnel had to wear Mission Oriented Protective Posture (MOPP) level four while on the base. MOPP level four is basically being covered head to toe in protective, chemical resistant garments issued by the Army. With temperatures well over a hundred and ten degrees daily, this was a miserable way to get around on base. Somehow the rest of Kuwait didn't get the memo of the threat, since no one else was wearing the gear or seemed to be phased by any threats of chemical weapons outside of the base. The contractors would leave Camp Doha, find a place to pull over so they could remove the MOPP gear, and would head downtown to a Starbucks street café (which are on every corner in the city) to drink a cappuccino.

Military members are not allowed to regularly leave the base freely without permission or good reason, so most of my social life in the beginning was spent with other American contractors living downtown. After work and on the weekends, I made an effort to get out into the city as often as possible. I was able to meet expats from other countries and grew a network of friends. The shopping malls were amazing and there were five within a thousand-meter radius of where I lived. Every price tag was changed from dollars to dinars, which meant that the same $19.00 music CD found in a mall in the US, was sold on the Kuwait retail market and marked to 19.00 KD, making the cost of the item three times more than what we would pay on the U.S. market. While everything was more expensive, pretty much anything we wanted could be found, we just had to be willing to pay for it.

The Radisson Hotel offered private yearly memberships, which gave me access to its private resort. It was useful and nice having a membership there to spend time on the weekends sitting by the pool in a bathing suit, and not worrying or being self-conscious about covering myself. With the resort being private, pretty much any bathing suit attire was acceptable. In some ways it didn't even feel like I was in a Muslim country anymore once I stepped through those gates. The public beaches weren't as flexible. They were divided into men-only and women-only beaches, as well as family beaches. Even with the specific designations for men, women, and family, there was still uncertainty about wearing Western beach attire. You might get away with it as a foreigner, but to me, it seemed disrespectful to the culture to be on a public beach in a bikini, while local women were swimming in full-body *abayas*. It was alarming the first time I saw a woman swimming in an *abaya*, and I looked twice to make sure she wasn't drowning. There were many women swimming in *abayas* and after the shock wore off, it seemed logical for the culture. After all, they couldn't exactly hit the beach, throw off their *abayas*, and dive into the water in their J. Crew bikinis. Although many Kuwaiti women were free to wear much of the same clothes (conservatively) that Western women did during that time, there was still an expectation of modesty enforced by family and culture. The modesty of clothing worn by Kuwaiti women was of varying degrees. Both Kuwaiti women and men told me that women have a choice on wearing a *hijab*—which just covered the hair—or not. Still, regardless of the level of modesty observed by the women, Western style bathing suits on public beaches weren't permitted.

The membership at the resort included access to indoor and outdoor pools, as well as a private beach. The resort also had yoga classes and gym facilities. It was a nice retreat to unwind and recharge on the weekends, and a great place to meet and connect with other expats living and working in the city.

Slowly, as time went on, my circle of American friends changed. There were some close friends that I kept and did regular social things with, such as trying new restaurants, shopping, visiting the souks, and going to expat-hosted private parties. But there were others who had less in common and fell away, as they weren't interested in doing any more than going to work and going directly home. They were simply happy with just doing what they came to do—*work*—and had little desire to go beyond.

Once connected with the Lebanese expats, it didn't take long to discover the underground party scene. From my experience, no matter where you are in the world, if you want to have a good time and find out where the party is, you just need to find the Lebanese community; they know how to have a party even in a dry country. They sold tickets to professionally DJ'ed private parties for 100 KD, which was about $300. With no taxes to pay, on top of the great expat salary, it didn't seem like much to enjoy dancing and the club scene for a night. It was less expensive than leaving the country, that's for sure. For another 100 KD, there were ways to find alcohol on the black market if you wanted to have drinks while attending the party. Groups of us went to these parties and enjoyed the drinks and dancing as a way to occasionally escape the normally quiet Kuwaiti social scene in the local coffee shop or restaurant. In the beginning, there was concern as to whether the party would be safe. All I needed was to get busted and end up in Kuwaiti prison. The party was cohosted by very rich Kuwaitis with high-level social connections, also known as "wastah" in the Kuwait government and police force, and Kuwaitis were actually at the party dancing and drinking with us.

At my first expat party, I was standing in line for the ladies' room. Two women in full *abayas* with their faces covered waited ahead of me. They went into the bathroom stall and, moments later, came out with their makeup and hair perfectly done and dressed for a night at the club.

They stepped in front of the mirror, refreshed their lipstick, and walked out, strutting like runway models, to enjoy the night without skipping a beat. Later I learned that perhaps they didn't want anyone to recognize them coming from the outside into the party, as it was taboo for Kuwaiti women to be out alone in those days dressed that way. Depending on their situation and the families that they came from, a night out could end pretty badly for them; it could ruin their reputations, and perhaps prevent them from finding suitable husbands. After all, Kuwait is a very small country.

Other than seeing an occasional Kuwaiti woman socially at a party, it was hard for me to connect with and meet Kuwaiti women in my age group at all while living in Kuwait. I was curious to understand more about their lives and what their views were, not only about their country, but also about America. They seemed to keep close to their circle of friends and family and, as an expat, it wasn't always easy to form friendships with them. Had I attended a college class or been involved with school activities with my daughter and their children, there would have been more opportunities. Having met some of the older generation of Kuwaiti women through their sons, and after experiencing their kindness and hospitality, it made me want to know more about younger generation Kuwaiti women, but it simply didn't happen while I was there.

After spending many months in Kuwait, some Americans got creative about getting alcohol into the country. There was the normal bootlegging strategy of taking a road trip to Basra in southern Iraq. Since the base was largely populated by the British military, there was no shortage of adult beverages and spirits. Often contractors would buy cases of alcohol and drive back over the border, prohibition style. Others discovered ways to make wine and beer in their homes from kits. If you bought pure grape juice (readily available at the local Sultan Center) and sugar, the Indian cashier was quick to tell you, "Don't forget the yeast!" While the method was well known and quite common, the wine tasted horrible and faithfully delivered a raging headache the next morning. Still, after several months in a dry country, a glass of wine is a glass of wine. Alcohol was also readily available at the embassies, and plenty of people attended embassy parties. Others discovered that they could have alcohol mailed to them through the APO system, even though doing so was risky. Being caught with alcohol could lead to termination, deportation, and, in some cases, imprisonment. Contractors who had been caught with beer and winemaking kits in their packages, which were scanned with x-ray machines through the APO mailroom, were then barred from base and terminated by the company.

One day, I car-pooled into work with a colleague and we were both running behind. He realized too late that he had forgotten to remove the APO box with a gallon of vodka that he had received the previous day from the backseat of the car. As we were pulling up to the security checkpoint, two cars were already locked in the barriers behind us getting ready to enter the gate, there was no way to back up or turn the car around. He said, "Oh my God, I forgot the box. There's a bottle of vodka in it!" "You idiot, you're going to get me sent home!" I exclaimed. My mind racing, I started unbuttoning my blouse. "Close the box up so it's hard to open and play it cool, and follow my lead, and don't act nervous or you'll blow it. I am NOT going home today." The knee-length skirt I was wearing that day quickly became a mini skirt as I hiked it up while stepping out of the SUV. With all three of the guards' full attention, I was center stage as I bent over the hood of the car and pretended to fumble with the latch under the hood. "I think I need a little bit of help fellas." Two of the three guards ran to my assistance. As I was joking around with them, pretending to open the hood like a show room model, stroking the side of the vehicle with my hand, showing off the motor, they chuckled and one said, "Damn, why can't all security checks be like this one?" The third guard was checking the inside of the car, talking with my colleague yet trying to see what I was doing with the other two guards. He quickly inspected the back seat, never opened the box on the floor, and just shut the door. I continued to pose. My colleague's jaw was literally on the ground, but he got into the swing of things. He turned to the third guard. "I'm not sure how I make it through the day with her," he said. "And she's always like this!" "You get work done with her around?" the guard asked, before shouting "all clear." The one guard who had opened the hood of the car asked for my phone number. I rolled my eyes at my colleague and whispered, "He's so lame you need to feel sorry for me, not him, we get plenty of work done." I scribbled a random phone number on the back of his business card, smiled, and handed it back to him. We both jumped back into the car. I started the engine and waved at them as we drove away. They all waved back and laughed as we drove onto the base. Turning to my colleague, I punched him in the arm as hard as I could. "We will never, ever again be that lucky in our lives. You better get your shit together." "Ouch! You go from sexy to sassy on the turn of a dime. I'm sorry, it was an accident. I couldn't have made it through that without you! You were awesome, I thought for sure we were toast," he said. "Yeah, well, I wasn't about to go down for your stupidity. I'm never riding with you again. In fact, I'll find another way home tonight." "You're mad at me?" he said. "Of course I'm mad at you. You have no idea what I'm sacrificing to be here, or what I'm trying to accomplish. Just stay away from me." I was angry that he had put me in that position. Had the guards found that alcohol, the story would be ending here. We would have both been barred for life from that base and sent home. My career flashed before my eyes in those moments, and from that point on, not many friendships continued with the people I worked with on base. It became necessary for me to separate career and personal life. Besides, it was such a small community, which thrived on true and false gossip alike, and the parties and alcohol became boring and uninteresting to me. I started commuting with a couple of dear friends who were trust-worthy and interested in being out and about in the city, and, because they stayed away from the negativity and pettiness, they stayed friends.

Like anything in life, every situation is what you make it. There were certainly mistakes made by me along the way, and plenty of bad judgment calls on my part. It was part of my growing process personally and professionally. Looking back, I'm not exactly proud of how I got myself out of the situation with the vodka. If it was my vodka, conceding and owning the mistake, I could take the hit, but there was no way it was right for me to go down for his indiscretion; the angels were with me that day. There was learning from that situation. After that incident, before driving in a car onto the military base, I would pre-check the car to ensure there were no forbidden items left behind by the other workers. It made me vigilant and maybe even paranoid to a degree, but the big lesson learned by me that day was to never allow my fate to sit in someone else's hands. We are all born with what we need to survive; we just need to learn how to use it when we need it.

The American contractors working in Camp Doha were people from all backgrounds, demographics, and age groups. It was a strange motley crew of people, an unlikely group of friends that found themselves there for all sorts of reasons. There was a younger guy in his early 20's, Greg, who worked with me and lived in the same housing complex. He was into the social scene in Kuwait and somehow managed to meet and date a local Kuwaiti girl. Traditional dating as we understand it in the U.S. didn't exist in those days in Kuwait, and the fact that the girl was only 18 or 19 years old and still living under her parents' roof, made this a serious and unlawful situation for everyone involved. As Greg was dropping off the girl at her house, he decided to walk her to the door and end the night with a kiss. Her brother came out of the house and caught them, and the encounter turned into a physical confrontation. Greg got his butt kicked in the front yard of the house. Picking himself up and getting back into his car, he then decided to go back by the house. His ego was bruised and he wanted to readdress the issue. The brother and father were now outside getting into their vehicles. A high-speed chase was on. He drove as fast as he could to get away, even attempting a little off-roading in the desert to try and lose them in the sand. Greg wasn't close to being an expert at desert driving and his company car was slammed from behind by the father's SUV. Greg finally got himself back on the road and headed toward the Army base, chased by the Kuwaiti father and son along with the Kuwaiti police, lights and sirens blaring. The country manager for the contracting company we worked for was called and the U.S. Embassy was notified. Everyone was in a race to get to that Army base. As Greg barreled into Camp Doha's main gate, he held up his hands, jumped out of the car, and yelled, "I'm an American! Help me! They are trying to kill me!" The guards, who initially drew down on the high speeding vehicle that was heading in their direction, signaled to Greg and he ran to safety. The guards kept the barriers up as the Kuwaiti father, son, and police arrived just behind him. They were all now locked and loaded in a draw down with American base security. The country manager for the company and the U.S. Embassy representatives arrived. They began discussing the confrontation with the Kuwaitis and then with Greg. The Kuwaiti family was taking their daughter to the doctor's to ensure she hadn't been de-flowered by the American, and Greg was in American custody, praying that she was still a virgin. When it was determined that she was still a virgin, everyone breathed a sigh of relief. However, the embassy recommended that he be out of the country within the next 24 hours because they could not guarantee his safety from the Kuwaiti father and son. Greg's presence at the family's home, without being invited by the men of the family, was considered wrong by cultural standards and the law. The family would be completely justified in their actions towards him. Legally, Greg had no leg to stand on and was lucky to be alive. So, the next day he was on the first available flight out of the country and everyone went back to business as usual with a little more understanding of the boundaries American men could not cross in their interactions with Kuwaiti women. From then on out, the men were advised to just avoid contact with Kuwaiti women altogether, for their own safety and for the Kuwaiti women's safety.

CHAPTER 5

Time Marches On

"We keep moving forward, opening new doors, and doing new things, because we're curious and curiosity keeps leading us down new paths."

— Walt Disney

My time in Kuwait City became easier and thus more enjoyable. Getting around became simpler as I settled in, became more familiar with where to find the things needed for everyday living, figured out the streets and found shortcuts around traffic jams. My new focus was on learning more about the culture and looking for things to do in the city, especially activities off of the beaten path of the regular mall scene, where many Americans spent their time.

On one occasion, I found an event taking place within a cultural center in Kuwait City. It was a Japanese ceremony of drums offered free to the public in an effort to bring some outside culture and diversity to the Kuwaitis. A friend and I arrived early and managed to get a couple of front row seats in the hall, which reminded me of my high school auditorium. The Japanese performer was a skilled drummer who had played in orchestras for such musicals as *The Lion King.* He walked onto the stage wearing a ceremonial wrap similar to what a sumo wrestler might wear. He was short, muscular, and toned. After waiting a long time for silence, he shouted, "May I begin?" With the first strike of the baton on the drum, I could feel the vibration throughout my entire body. The sounds were quite loud, each one unique, and each strike resonated, shaking me from the inside out. His movements were graceful and seemed effortless. Hearing, feeling, and seeing his performance was mesmerizing. When he finished, the audience seemed awestruck, remaining silent until they remembered to start clapping.

I began to appreciate that experiences in my life were my best teachers. Some of my most fascinating memories were made in the most unlikely places — an unassuming hole in the wall eatery, or an out of the way shop. There were many such places in Kuwait. These off-the-beaten-path places were almost always where I found the best events or food and the most interesting people working or dining.

There were also the larger, fancier, and popular shopping malls, which were filled with many common brands. Shopping for women's clothing was often difficult for me because my height and size meant that the clothes offered, which were designed for smaller Asian women, would not fit. My shoulders were too broad for shirts and my American thighs wouldn't squeeze into the pants. If my thighs could get into the pants the waist would be too wide. The tags had sizes in almost every language except English. Size 16 pants fit me, but in the U.S. I typically wore a size ten.

Western women mostly wore whatever they wanted, with the styles tending towards mildly conservative, with short sleeves and showing not too much cleavage. Shorts, capris, and knee-length skirts seemed okay. Really short shorts or short skirts were rarely seen in those days. Most women preferred to cover their skin anyway for protection against the blazing sun. Looser cotton clothing that breathed well was what most people wore. The sun was so intense at times that people often demonstrated the heat by cooking eggs on the sidewalk. The rubber on the bottom of my cheap shoes got sticky from walking down the street.

The water tanks for the apartments were on the roof, sitting in the hot sun, which made it difficult to take a cool shower until evening, when sunset cooled things down. At times, when trying to take a shower, the cold water coming from the tap was hotter than the hot water. The heat was indeed something that took some getting used to.

I developed a taste for the culture and a feel for the city as a result of visiting the various souks, or open markets, mostly in the evenings because of the heat. It didn't take us long to learn about shopping in Hawali's electronic district for instance, where we could find the best prices for every type and brand of electronics. Discovering the best places to get the things we needed became part of the fun of being there as expats. It was almost like a scavenger hunt. Often, we would trade notes on where to go for what, and to whom to talk to for the best deal. We quickly learned that in the Arab culture, business is relationship-based, so bringing friends to a vendor over and over again is good for the customers, but also builds a relationship with the merchant. It's more than just exchanging money for the product and then business is over. There a trust-based business relationship is built over exchanging words, sitting down for tea, coffee, or juice, and establishing rapport. Westerners often make the mistake of taking their way of conducting business to the Middle East, and their heavy handedness often backfires. I've personally watched Americans get raked over the coals or blow a deal completely because they simply were too ego-driven or stubborn to adapt. Anyone wanting to do business in the Middle East should try to understand some basic principles of the culture. It's like a dance of personal understanding and in reality, most Westerners just needed to know not to turn down the offer of tea, and to willingly sit and learn about the person with whom they were doing business.

Along with my American friend, Shane, I took frequent trips to the computer software and hardware places in the electronics district in Hawali. Shane was quite a bit older and shorter than I was, a grey haired, stereotypical looking computer geek with a round belly that required him to wear red suspenders in order to keep his pants up, along with thick glasses so he could see. The rumor mill at work was in full effect with tales that we were having an affair. We both laughed at the assumptions and decided never to correct the ridiculously wild accusations people were making. We actually became great friends. He was always up for an adventure, would try any restaurant I took him to, and his clever wit and humor always kept me in stitches. The only thing Shane would not do is drive in Kuwait, as he found the experience terrifying. In fact, that's how our friendship started. He had a company car and was willing to be my wingman while I entertained him with my cultural and dating adventures. In return, I was his driver, willing to take on any traffic situation in Kuwait, even the bumper-to-bumper madness of Hawali. Maybe an odd looking friendship from the outside, but it worked and I appreciated being friends with a guy who had no agenda.

While in Hawali one night, a rather rotund and jolly Kuwaiti man approached us. Speaking casually to us in his shop for several minutes, he then asked Shane, "Would you and your wife please join me for some juice or tea in my office? I would like to show you some new products going to market in London and potentially in the U.S. Ma'am you will be fascinated by the largest-cut emerald in the region in my possession." "My darling, how could one turn down such brilliance?" I replied looking at Shane, who was trying hard not to laugh. We followed the man into his office, and he asked a small Indian boy to bring us back juice and tea. The Kuwaiti man opened his briefcase, making sure that we saw his 9mm pistol and handcuffs, equipment supplied to police officers from the criminal investigation division. The black market in Kuwait was alive and well and there was no telling if the guy was really a police officer or just trying to impress us because he had the equipment. It was illegal for civilians in that part of the world to possess guns or handcuffs. Needless to say, it was a bizarre way to start a business conversation.

Shane was visibly uncomfortable and once the beverages arrived, I wondered if they were safe to drink. I pretended to take a tiny sip now and then while he spoke about the new technology he had found that allowed him to print tiny holographic portraits of people on gold plates. He planned to make necklaces out of the miniature portraits and sell them. Each time I tried to ask a question, he would interrupt me, "But ma'am please, just listen to what I'm telling you. This is the best, most original piece of jewelry you will find in the world." Shane, sat up straight looking at his watch, "Ah, umm, well, ugh yea, it could be lucrative but we're computer people, not sales people, and we need to get going now. I need to put my wife to bed or she'll get cranky." "Wait, wait what about the emerald," I said, changing the subject. The man ducked behind a curtain and came back carrying a long, floor-length, dark velvet dress. Awkwardly attached to the front of the dress was the largest-cut emerald I had ever seen, a little smaller than a baseball. Besides the emerald, there were other jewels mounted on the front and back of the dress. He pointed out small rubies, diamonds, and several yellow garnets the size of a half dollar. He explained that the dress was by a famous designer in Kuwait to showcase his jewel collection, worn by only the most beautiful models in fashion shows. I asked if the dress was too heavy to wear. "Ma'am please," he retorted. "Fashion models don't care about how heavy." Sensing that things had gone on long enough, Shane stood up, thanked the man for his time, congratulated him on his great fashion sense, and let him know we would think about his business ideas. We sat in the car for a moment laughing so hard we cried. What had just transpired? My attempts to have a normal conversation on the drive home were diverted by Shane in his best Kuwaiti accent saying, "But ma'am please, ..." which would send me into a fit of hysterics.

My life in Kuwait was full of interesting and memorable interactions. It's hard to explain how easy it is living there, if pre-conceived notions of the difficulties of living in the Middle East exist. However, with the company taking care of all the housing needs, and pretty much every convenience available and attainable for a price, it made for a good quality of life. At the same time, I needed to guard against becoming too complacent, taking safety for granted. It was common to be driving in the city after a long day of shopping with an expat female friend and realize that Kuwaiti men were following us home. We would try to lose them by driving around, but if that didn't work, we'd have to call a male co-worker to meet us at the grocery store parking lot a few blocks from the housing complex. As soon as a man joined us, his presence would scare away even the most persistent guy. We didn't want droves of random men knowing where we lived. Aside from terrorism, in America that kind of behavior is called stalking. Among the younger generation in Kuwait, driving by a woman's residence was a pretty common way that younger men pursued women since approaching them outright in public was frowned upon. So they flirted with each other from one car to another while driving down Arab Gulf Road, hoping to trade cell phone numbers. It was common to see the young men showing off their nice cars and motorcycle tricks while trying to get the attention of a girl. (In the U.S., older generations called this "cruising.") Once a man obtained a woman's number, the text messaging would begin. In fact, text messages were a major part of how people communicated with each other in Kuwait, even as far back as 2003. Text messaging didn't gain popularity in the U.S. until well after 2006. In some ways the Kuwaitis seemed so behind, but in other ways they were a little more advanced and clever with using technology to their advantage. Despite the older generation's repressive social rules, the younger generation found another way to circumvent the stale Arab traditions, using technology to do what humans have long done with one another, which is to connect.

One night, while sitting at a traffic light talking to some male coworkers who were in the vehicle with me, I looked over and caught the eye of a very handsome Kuwaiti man. The light changed and we drove away. He met us again at the next light. My coworkers said, "He's staring at you. Look!" He was handsome and he smiled warmly at me, and I quickly looked away. We played this cat and mouse game at each traffic light all the way through Kuwait City and back to our apartments. The guys in the car were roaring with laughter, making jokes how if I dated him he would make me wear the black "ninja outfit," the *abaya*. One coworker admitted that he was worried that I was even considering talking to him. Shane quickly piped in, "I'm pretty sure it's him we need to worry about, not her. She can handle herself." They all laughed and agreed he might be right. Most of the Americans I worked with were content never to interact or be involved with the Kuwaiti people or culture, so the fact that this was happening with a local seemed radical to the others riding in the car. Looking in my rear view mirror, I noticed that he had pulled off in front of the *bakala*, or convenience store, in our neighborhood. After parking the car, my colleagues went into our apartment building and I walked across the street to the *bakala*. I decided to approach him, still unsure of what I would say. The lightly tinted window on his black Land Rover slowly lowered. He smiled while extending his hand to shake mine, and we introduced ourselves. He said his name was Mohammed, a fairly common name given to Arab males after the well-known Islamic prophet. We chatted for a few minutes and I asked him, "There was a car full of men with me, why did you think it was okay to follow me home? Normally, having men with me scares Kuwaiti men away" "But you are American, yes?" I nodded. "You are a woman driving the car for three men. What kind of men are these, ones that I should be worried about?" he asked. I didn't smile, but he did. "You have pretty eyes. What is the color?" he asked, peering intently into my eyes. "Thank you, they are green." "I've never seen that, green eyes. They are very pretty. Mostly, we all have brown eyes." Feeling a little shy and looking away at a car passing by I said, "Ah, thanks. You have pretty eyes, too, actually. Brown eyes are nice." After a moment of silence, he asked for my phone number. I handed him my cell phone and he typed his number into my phone and sent a text message, while explaining that he was supposed to be running an errand for his sister and the detour to meet me made him a little late. He asked if he could take me out sometime, and I said yes. I saw no harm in meeting up with him again, still curious about the local people my age. After agreeing when to meet, we said goodbye.

Turning around to walk back towards my apartment, I noticed that two Indian security guards for our building had been peering around the corner, watching our exchange. They quickly scattered once they realized they were caught. They were as intrigued as anyone else at what was happening. It was exciting for me, not only because he was handsome and charming, but also because it had been a while since I'd been on a real date with anyone. There was still a chip on my shoulder about my divorce and being in a relationship was not of any interest to me, the healing process still needed to unfold. Still, dating made me feel somewhat normal again; it felt new and exciting. It was a good time to go meet people, have fun, and enjoy my surroundings without any pressure.

I went out with Mohammed several times over the period of a few months. Logistics were a problem since he was very much into the nightlife, working in the evenings at the airport as a supervising immigration officer and then sleeping most of the day. On the base most of us worked a normal Monday through Friday schedule, with an eight-hour day. As he was getting up to start his day, I was just leaving work and making dinner plans for six or seven o'clock at night, which is a pretty early dinner by Kuwaiti standards.

Usually, we met up on the weekends or later in the evenings. He took me to a few traditional restaurants he liked and introduced me to *shisha*, a three-foot tall Arabic water pipe with sweetened and flavored regular tobacco. There was a wide array of fruit-flavored tobaccos to choose from, like cherry, grape, and apple, as well as mint. While the tobacco was smooth and tasted nice, smoking gave me the most unpleasant headache in the morning, and made my throat feel like I'd gone through a couple of packs of cigarettes. He took me on beautiful wooden fishing ships on the water, where most locals went, and showed me *souks* where I could buy the best and freshest fish, spices, and vegetables. He also showed me the best way to negotiate for gold and where to find the best seamstresses and tailors to make custom clothes from the finest fabrics in Asia. He was an excellent tour guide, showing me things in a way I could have never figured out to see alone.

He was easy to talk to and respectful. Over time, however, he started to say things to me that seemed kind of bossy and ridiculous, and his comments rubbed me the wrong way. In my mind we were just hanging out as a friends, not a serious thing to me, and surely not serious enough for him to be telling me what to do. He was very forthright about how he viewed the dynamics between a man and woman. "The man is the man," he said, explaining further, "In Kuwait, a man can do anything without being questioned by a woman, even if it's deemed inappropriate." Rolling my eyes and laughing, I said, "You aren't serious?" "Yes, of course this is true for my culture." His ideas were absurd to me, but at the same time I was curious whether he was truly living this way with the women in his family, or just a big talker trying to see what he could get away with saying to me.

He eventually took me to meet his sisters and his father, who had just had surgery. Both of his sisters were very beautiful and wore *hijabs*. Sitting with them, they offered me coffee and the small chocolate sweets commonly served with coffee. After I finished my coffee, Mohammed continued to offer me additional sweets, all of which I politely declined. The more I declined, the more he tried to convince me to eat more. Having just eaten prior to showing up there, and already full from our meal, I didn't want more. He finally conceded, mumbling something in Arabic and shaking his head. His sister smiled politely at me and said, "You are a very strong woman." "I'm just totally full from the meal we ate before we got here. Please excuse me," I said apologetically. "I completely understand," she said. "Our culture loves nothing more than to continuously feed our guests. Sometimes it can be overwhelming." We began chatting and, having been educated in the United Kingdom, she spoke perfect English. She earned her degree in dentistry from a university in Ireland. She also told me a bit about her travels in the U.S., Canada, and Great Britain. She asked me about my career, my family, and about my impressions living in Kuwait. She said she hoped that it wasn't boring for me in Kuwait and that her brother was being a proper host, showing me around and keeping me entertained.

As soon as Mohammed left the room, she lowered her voice, turned to face me, looked me in the eye, and quickly said, "My brother is always angry and you should be careful with him." Since I had yet to see that side of him, I was shocked. But the look in her eye told me that she was serious and concerned. Not knowing how to respond, I just nodded my head and sipped my coffee.

There were things he said and did that seemed a bit overbearing, like telling me to be home and in bed by ten p.m. Sometimes, there was uncertainty whether he was being serious or kidding. Mostly I laughed it off and reassured him that, of course, I would be home and in bed at the right time. This, of course, was the beginning of the end of our time together. As much as I enjoyed seeing things around the city with him, the cultural disparity between us was starting to become more and more difficult to look past. The more he pushed things, the more my resistance toward him and his antics rose to the surface. After going through the divorce, I knew what I wanted my position as a woman to be. His mindset and behavior, whether it was cultural, blatant male chauvinism, or just immature jealousy, made being with him no longer a fun or exciting experience.

He would get frustrated with our conversations and tell me that the problem with American women was that they are too strong, specifically that I was too strong and unpredictable. To sort out the unpredictable issue, he insisted that I text him upon arrival to work, and then again when leaving work, and then yet again when arriving at home. Often, he would be waiting at my apartment when I arrived. He said he wanted to ensure my safety. The attention was flattering in the beginning, but his over-played attentiveness became an annoyance to me, and the checking in requests were the kisses of death for our friendship. It wasn't a door slammed in your face kind of good-bye; slowly, I stopped meeting him, blaming a busy work schedule, and he stopped texting me, or inviting me to come out. It was a sensitive situation. I had to be careful not to do anything that would create trouble for me entering or leaving the country. With his position as an immigration officer at the airport, it was best to keep him as a friend. Besides, in Kuwait it never hurts to have a little of your own *wastah* (connections).

Ramadan, which started around the beginning of October, was a couple of days away, which meant that Mohammed would spend more time with his family that month, particularly in the evenings when breaking the fast. Ramadan is celebrated on the nineteenth month of the

Islamic lunar calendar.[6] I would say that all Muslims fast during daylight hours, however no one knows what goes on behind closed doors, and for each person, fasting is a personal journey. In public however, during the daylight hours, fasting began around five a.m., the *zoluq* time. At that time, the roads, sidewalks, and coffee shops would be empty with the city looking like a ghost town. The exceptions were the retail shops in the mall that didn't sell food items and were open because the workers were expats, not Kuwaitis. Food places and cafes were closed until the official *iftar* time, usually around sunset (these times shift depending on time of year that Ramadan falls on), which meant that even the non-Muslims and expats living in Kuwait had to observe this period as well. No eating, drinking, or even smoking in public was allowed, and, if caught, violators could be arrested. For Muslims, the fast is considered a period to self-sacrifice, focus on the worship of God, and realign life with religious principles. Muslims strive to make peace with self or any former external altercations, get away from bad habits, and reunite with family. It's an overall purification period of the mind, body, and soul. Reading about it when I first got there, it reminded me of a spiritual rebirthing process. Perhaps emerging from this period made them feel renewed somehow or better than before. It seemed like a useful practice if it could be followed with those intentions. On Camp Doha, it was business as usual; there was no fasting requirement on the base. However, we were warned daily to avoid taking even a sip of water or a bite of food while driving down the road,

---

[6] http://islam.about.com/od/ramadan/f/ramadanintro.htm

and not to smoke or chew gum in public because it was forbidden during this period. There were rumors of a couple of soldiers being arrested for smoking outside the mall downtown during Ramadan, and the military reps had to negotiate their prison release after a day or two. Normally, if arrested for this infraction, a person would stay in prison until Ramadan was over. Kuwait jails do not provide food to prisoners, so if someone is arrested and goes to prison, they must depend on friends to supply food. American federal prisons seem like nice accommodations compared to the conditions in the Kuwaiti prisons.

Despite the Kuwaiti government amending the workday to half days during Ramadan, the drives home were even crazier than usual. Those drivers fasting all day starving, thirsty, and, if a smoker, experiencing nicotine withdrawal during those drives, were rushing home to break the fast with their families. Tempers on the road flared and cars driven by men in *dishdashas* weaved through traffic, ignoring all traffic laws and blowing through red lights. Driving during this period certainly required complete alertness and extremely defensive driving skills. Once fasters were home with the family and the fast was broken, there was a huge feast and everyone celebrated, eating and drinking all evening long. Once the sun rose, the observance began again, and the cycle went on for about 30 days. Most people stayed in and slept during the day, including the government workers, so it was exceptionally problematic to get anything done in an official capacity during this period. The country practically stopped; even banks had reduced hours. Ramadan ended with *Eid al-Fitr*, the festival of breaking the fast and the end of the spiritual reflection. They had a ceremony, ate dates, offered charity to the poor, spent time with family and remembered those who had passed, all while celebrating life.

Ramadan being a big part of the culture, it was understandably important for Mohammed to be with his family. Once this period began, our friendship faded and we didn't see each other socially again.

I saw Mohammed in the airport several months later and debated if or how I would approach him. I was traveling with a friend to Dubai for the weekend. As soon as we made eye contact, he left his podium and walked down the long line of people to where we were waiting. He smiled, reached out his hand to take mine, and we kissed on each other's cheeks like old friends, as typically seen in Kuwait. "All the women that work for me will be gossiping now about the beautiful American woman I kissed in the airport," he said, smiling. "How are you doing, *Habibi*?" "Doing great, thank you," I said. "It's nice to see you here. How is your family?" "They are all fine. My sister was asking about you, hoping you get along here fine. Listen, next time you come to the airport, text me so you don't ever wait in the line. Okay, follow me." He gestured for us to follow him and walked us to the front of the long line of people patiently waiting. We handed our passports to him and he typed something into the computer and stamped each one. Handing back our passports, he said goodbye, winked at me, and we waved goodbye. My friend was laughing as we walked away. "Leave it to you to find a hook-up with a Kuwaiti immigration official," she said. "How do you know that guy?" "We went on a few dates once and I met his family. Once the novelty of dating each other wore off, we went our separate ways, no harm no foul apparently." It seemed the easiest way to explain what had transpired between us without hashing through the details.

Dating him and living in Kuwait gave me context to make comparisons about our cultures. The observations made me realize that Western women do have opportunities denied to women in other parts of the world. We can vote, have careers, and choose whether or not to get married or have children. We don't have to worry about disgracing the family if we have premarital sex or don't get married at the right time in life. I think a lot of young women in Western cultures take these differences for granted.

I learned a lot about myself—what I liked and didn't like, for the most part—through the experience of living abroad. I learned what I could put up with in my life, and what simply would not do, what my strengths and weaknesses were, and the areas where I lacked flexibility and tolerance for others, especially for other cultures. Some of my preconceptions and judgments were misdirected. Over time, some misconceptions were overruled by my experiences while other notions were confirmed.

In Kuwait, my misconceptions about women were oftentimes widely overturned, as many women were highly educated and spoke better English than most of the men, yet it was interesting to see how they were still under the thumb of older brothers, husbands, and fathers. Imagine how much further evolved every society could be if women contributed to society in the way they wanted, instead of the way that is expected; it would require men to lighten up a bit. Even men who were educated or had spent time living in America or Europe had difficulty changing their attitudes about women, perhaps because these attitudes were deeply steeped in their cultural beliefs. I respect the cultural beliefs of Kuwait and liked aspects of the culture that I experienced. However, there were parts of the culture that seemed to hold women back from their greatest potential, limiting the gifts and contributions that could be made by women to child rearing and being wives. Then again, there are versions of those same inequities right here in America. Regardless of the cultural differences or similarities, there doesn't seem to be a gap between what makes us all decent human beings at the core of who we are.

With Thanksgiving around the corner, the weather in Kuwait became increasingly colder. In the winter months the Gulf wind can be fierce, cutting through like a knife. People gathered more often inside homes and spent less time doing activities outside in the evenings. My social life was full of things to do, meeting and spending time with expats from other countries working in Kuwait. I met people from the United Kingdom, Eastern Europe, and others from the Middle East region. For me, connecting with these new groups of people from all over the globe meant an even more interesting cultural expansion.

One particular friend from Macedonia, Angelina, loved having gatherings at her house and preparing wonderful feasts of Macedonian and American food for all of our friends. She insisted on holding the Thanksgiving feast at her house and prepared a full range of traditional holiday dishes from the Mediterranean and America. There were eight Macedonian women there with their husbands, a few Americans we worked with, and some local Kuwaiti friends. An Arab-looking man showed up after everyone else had arrived and, after Angelina introduced him to me, I learned his name was Waleed. It almost felt like a set up. Shaking his hand, we exchanged greetings and he quickly went to sit down on the other side of the room. He was very quiet, mostly observing everyone around him. Helping Angelina with the food, I didn't go out of my way to say much to him. I remained jaded about Muslim men from my interactions with Mohammad and was quite content with being single. As the night went on, people started to leave, and soon just a few of us were left at the party. We started discussing the nuances of the Kuwaiti culture and laughing about some of the silly differences between various cultures around the world.

Charles, Angelina's husband, got a call from a friend in the States and went into another room to talk. After a few minutes, Angelina followed him. I found myself alone with Waleed. Looking at me, he said, "You know, we are not all bad, and some of us do respect women and think they are to be cherished." I was speechless. He hadn't spoken two words to me since he shook my hand hours ago and now he was calling me out directly on my negative attitude and beliefs about Arab men. Not knowing what to say, I nodded my head slowly, and acknowledged that yes, there were probably plenty of men that had been raised to think women had value. We talked for a while longer, and he began to tell me about his childhood, how his father died when he was at a very young age, and how his mother, aunts, and uncles raised him. He talked about his love for his mother, remarking on her strength and how he respected her for everything she went through to raise him without his father. As the night started to wind down, he asked if he could take me out for dinner some time. Unsure about that and maybe still unready, I said, "Maybe sometime," with a smile.

A few days later, Angelina sent me a text message asking if she could give my number to Waleed because he had asked her for it. She followed up that request with another text. "I know what you're thinking, but he's a nice guy. Stop being foolish and go to dinner with him." Caving in, I let her give my number to him and within a few hours Waleed made contact with me. There were days of text messages and phone calls, and we became friends. He was patient, sensing my hesitation, but we finally went to dinner and had a great time. He loved being out in the city and trying new restaurants and cafés as much as I did. We went to sushi restaurants, Italian and Indonesian restaurants, and to beautiful resorts with amazing dining. He took me to private parties, and there was also plenty of the ever-forbidden wine and other types of alcohol there. It was so good to have a real glass of wine from a bottle imported from Lebanon or Italy. I was starting to get too used to the homemade wines and alcohol made locally by the underground expat bootleggers. The imported wine was very welcomed.

Soon after meeting him, Waleed started to introduce me to his friends and other expats living and working in Kuwait. They were around our age, single, and fun to hang around and talk to. After meeting and talking with people from all over the world, they mostly came to Kuwait for the same reason I did: they were following a career, trying to make more money, and were ready for new adventures.

Waleed soon introduced me to his mother, a sweet and gentle woman. She was a schoolteacher and an amazing cook. She cooked dinners for us with the help of the two maids that lived with them. She always said she thought I was too skinny and didn't think I could possibly be eating enough because my family wasn't there. A woman after my heart! The first time Waleed invited me for dinner, the amount of food on the table was unbelievable. Asking him who was eating dinner with us, he shook his head and said it was just us; whispering that his mother sometimes went overboard when she cooked for him. The table, with enough seating for twenty, was covered with a variety of Arabic foods, like *kibbi*, a ground meat dish, lamb chops, *tabouli* a parsley and bulgur wheat salad, *hummus* ground chick peas with oil and tahini, fresh flat bread, *fatoush* a type of salad, stuffed potatoes, rice dishes, a mix of grilled meats, salads dressed with oil and lemon, baklava for desserts, and too many other dishes to name. It felt like we were at the Last Supper!

After Waleed sat down, I opted to sit at his left side directly next to him. We ate as much as we could but it seemed like every time we took a bite of something the maid would bring something else out for me to try. Finally, I gave up without trying everything, I couldn't eat one more bite. We stepped out onto his covered stone patio where one of the house staff was tending a small fire. We sat in a love seat that was in front of the fireplace. He kept asking me if everything was okay, if I needed anything else. I told him that a coffee would be wonderful. Before the sentence left my lips, he called to his driver, a petit Indian man, and instructed him to go to Starbucks. Ten or fifteen minutes later, he returned carrying two tall coffees. Waleed slipped him some cash and the man nodded his head and disappeared into the villa. As we talked and finished our coffee, he wanted to show me around his family's house, noting it was the American thing to do. The tour was quite long because the house was truly a mansion. He took me around the bottom and main levels; the kitchen was amazing, resembling an upscale restaurant kitchen. The counter space was endless and there were three refrigerators. We walked into the living room as he explained the layout of the home. He pushed a button and two doors opened with a loud "ding." I gasped in disbelief. "An elevator? What do you need that for?" Since the family lived mostly on the first floor, it seemed bizarre, not to mention lazy, using an elevator to go up one flight of stairs, but we did. Upstairs he showed me another informal living area where all the furniture was trimmed in sterling silver and gold. In fact, all of the bathroom fixtures, including the toilet seat, were gold-plated as well. Imagine my amazement walking into the bathroom and realizing I was about to sit on a gold-plated toilet seat! He pointed to the top third and fourth floors where the maids lived. I was interested in what their living conditions looked like. It always seemed a little strange to me that most Kuwaiti families had maids and nannies that were either Filipina or Indian women and were made to wear ugly uniforms that looked like over-sized pajamas. I visually studied how the two classes interacted because of the endless stories of abuse and trafficking we heard about these foreign workers. I was never able to confirm any of the stories with my own experience or interactions. However, there was a noticeable difference in the way they spoke down to the nanny, maid, or driver, versus how they treated each other.

As we rounded the corner to another area of the home, we walked into his ridiculously huge bedroom. The immediate area was a sitting area with a coffee table and a large screen TV with an amazing surround sound system. The next area looked like an office space with bookshelves, a computer desk, a few computers, and a swivel chair. In the far area was a king-sized bed and a walk-in closet. The walk-in closet alone was the size of my bedroom, about twelve-feet by thirteen-feet. Everything was neatly organized and arranged by season and color, right down to every T-shirt, sneaker, and Italian leather dress shoe. His entire bedroom was only about two hundred feet smaller than the home I had back in North Carolina.

He was a very soft and gentle guy and we stayed platonic friends during my time there. He was exactly what I needed at that time in my life. He didn't pressure me, he was easy to be around, and he liked doing nice things for me. There were times he sent his driver over to pick me up for the day so that I wouldn't have to drive to do my shopping and run errands. Also he dropped off one of his cars for me to borrow when my company car was in the shop or being borrowed by someone else. He looked out for me when I needed something or was sick. Always a gentleman and very respectful, he changed my sweeping beliefs about Arab people, particularly my opinion about Kuwaiti men. I knew he wanted more from me though, and he made it clear that after a certain amount of time seeing someone, that it would be appropriate to discuss marriage. My comments about marriage included stories of my two failed marriages and my intentions not to rush into another marriage anytime soon.

Living in Kuwait for the rest of my life was not an option, and he couldn't leave the business that he ran for his family to move to the United States. We spent some good moments together; having a great friend was helpful and made my life pleasant. Knowing I didn't love him, something else inside of me wouldn't let me give him a chance at anything more. There was still a lot of unsettled emotional turmoil from my past that I was trying to work out and make sense of. On top of that I was still trying to figure out who I was and where to be in my life. Nothing felt settled or complete, and feeling the pressures and expectations that would come with a relationship created anxiety for me. Closing my eyes, thinking about my life, I still didn't see myself with him or with anyone else for that matter. Besides, there were still more fabulous adventures, and more interesting places to see!

Nothing in or about Kuwait or the Middle East seemed scary to me after that point. I realized that the things I believed, thought, or was told about that part of the world, Arab culture, and especially Arab people, might not be completely accurate. The people in my prior community could be wrong and the perceptions that the TV and media perpetuated and portrayed could be wrong. I felt welcomed with open arms by everyone I ran into, and was shown exquisite hospitality and willingness to share their culture as a fellow human being and friend. Kuwaitis were proud and courteous to show me their way of life, and were curious and respectful of mine. Of course, I didn't live as a daughter or wife in this country and so perhaps my opinion is also biased from that perspective. Women in Kuwait weren't allowed to vote until 2006. There are certainly plenty of documented cases of injustice towards women as well. Indeed, the Kuwaitis, just like so many other cultures, are people with very different cultural mindsets, customs, and belief systems. Showing respect and curiosity for the culture while attempting to withhold my judgments is probably what made my experience there a great one. The mindset of how you approach a culture makes all the difference in the world. I believe that if it's gone into with a level of thinking that you know a better way or your culture is right, then you will be full of criticism for the way things are done. They are still humans with the same human desires and needs as all humans have. They have the same basic need to love and to feel loved. They experience a love for their family; they love their mothers and fathers, their brothers and sisters and other extended family members. They go on vacations, and they go grocery shopping. They feel fear, anger, sadness, and all the other emotions humans encounter. That is not a society that hates the entire Western world. Though some people might feel that way, I would argue that we probably have as many Christians with similarly negative beliefs about Muslims. The situation and contention that has been, and continues to be experienced, as unrest in the Middle East and other places in the world is not exactly a religious problem; this is lack of heart, respect, and compassion perpetuated by misinformation and intolerance of humans, cultures, and beliefs, perhaps on both sides. When do the media show the educated, everyday people of the Middle East living their lives in peace, loving each other, having normal life experiences? Where are the stories about Arab families watching their children graduate high school or play sports, about babies being born, people falling in love, and celebrating weddings? Where are the happy everyday stories? Not every Arab person you see has malicious intention and hate, or is out to do something terrible to America. Since the media only shows Muslims performing horrifying acts, the shape and suggestion of the message begins to look like one big sweeping belief that all "Muslims" are against us and therefore are terrorists. I'm not suggesting that terrorism isn't real or is not happening, but that there is danger in broad, gross generalizations and thinking that one group of people is all one way or another. This way of thinking separates us, creating an "us" against "them" mentality. No matter what beliefs a person has or what faith they follow, we are all one human family first, and that should count for something far more substantial than where you were born, what shade of brown your skin is or isn't, and which version of God you choose to worship or believe.

CHAPTER 6

Beliefs

"Beliefs are like commanders of the brain. When we congruently believe something is true, it is like delivering a command to our brain as to how to represent what is occurring."

— Tony Robbins

Beliefs are important because they not only shape our convictions, but they lend understanding of how to make sense of our lives, and affect our views of the world around us. Living far away, safe in my small-town Maine community where my only knowledge of Middle Eastern culture was what was seen on the evening news or heard from other people's opinions, my beliefs and understanding were truly myopic and limited. It took a great deal of effort for me to remain open-minded and curious without judging others while living in the Middle East. Despite my willingness to replace old beliefs with new ones, I found the process challenging but ultimately beneficial, enabling me to make a rich and exciting lifestyle while living abroad. Without an eagerness to leave certain beliefs behind, I would have lost out on many good friendships that softly encouraged me to begin healing from my past, not to mention losing out on the priceless education of a new culture and religion that became a part of my daily life. Not everyone had the same reality as I did while living in Kuwait. We all get to choose how we experience life. Ultimately losing the old understanding allowed me to adopt a greater appreciation for the culture and the people I met along the way.

There are many definitions of beliefs. *Merriam-Webster* defines a belief as, "A feeling of being sure that someone or something exists or that something is true."[7] I like the definition parsed from the *Stanford Encyclopedia of Philosophy* and other sources in Wikipedia[8], "Belief is a mental representation, treated in various academic disciplines, especially philosophy and psychology, of a sentient being's attitude toward the likelihood or truth of something. In Greek, two different concepts are often represented by the concept of belief: Pistis and Doxa. Simplified we may say that the first deals in trust and confidence, the latter in opinion and acceptance." Basically, a mental representation or thoughts (energy) and emotions (more energy) toward that something, which may or may not be true, make-up a belief.

Throughout our history, society has held many beliefs; some beliefs have been right and others wrong. One example is the well-known but incorrect belief of the first scientists that the earth was flat and that the sun rotated around the earth. Galileo, who is credited with the construction of a

---

[7] http://www.merriam-webster.com/dictionary/beliefs
[8] https://en.wikipedia.org/wiki/Belief

telescope and supported the Copernican Theory, which is based on a sun-centered solar system, was accused twice of heresy by the Catholic Church for his beliefs and then imprisoned. The Copernican Theory was the opposite of the Geocentric Model, which the Church staunchly held onto as the divine hierarchy of humanity and order of the Universe, placing earth at the center of the Universe. Galileo challenged and eventually changed society's beliefs with his theories and ideas, but not before he got thrown in the slammer. Beliefs are powerful, especially widely held societal beliefs, because they make-up the framework and basis for society's collective reality. When that reality gets shaken, people start to get nervous, and it can be very upsetting to find out that something you always believed to be true is actually false because it begs the next question: what else could be false?

Just because a majority of people believe something doesn't make the belief truer. Conversely, just because very few people believe something doesn't mean it's likely to be false. We have all been programed with information, ideas, and perceptions that we maybe never challenged or doubted. Information that we believe to be true or false contributes to how we view life and go after life's experiences. Information is constantly being integrated into our belief systems, reinforced by media, our parents and schooling, and makes up the foundation of each of our realities, both national and world views.

Larger-scale beliefs feed "group consciousness." It's the resonance of the beliefs amongst a group that makes up the group consciousness, creating a basis for societal rules, ethics, and structures. There are plenty of examples of group consciousness throughout history. In Neale Donald Walsch's *Conversations with God, Book Two*[9], he relates two extreme examples of group consciousness, which he calls "collective consciousness." He speaks to Christ-like consciousness and then to Hitler's collective consciousness movement used to influence the German citizens to eradicate the Jewish people and take over Europe, eventually leading to World War II. "You see, it was collective consciousness which provided fertile soil for the growth of the Nazi movement. Hitler seized the moment, but he did not create it. It's important to understand the lesson here. A group consciousness which speaks constantly of separation and superiority produces loss of compassion on a massive scale, and loss of compassion is inevitably followed by loss of conscience," Walsch writes. He goes on to describe, "The consciousness of separation, segregation, a superiority of 'we' versus 'they' or 'us' and 'them' is what creates the Hitler Experience. The consciousness of the Divine Brotherhood, of unity, of Oneness, of 'ours' rather than 'yours' or 'mine,' is what creates the Christ Experience. When the pain is 'ours,' not just 'yours,' when the joy is 'ours,' not just 'mine,' when the whole life experience is Ours, then it is at last truly that – a Whole Life experience."

Living abroad and having so many of my personal beliefs turned upside down started me down a path of personal review, where other held beliefs were questioned, especially group-supported beliefs. There are beliefs and agreements that had certainly been made by me without much thought; I think there are beliefs and agreements that

---

[9] Walsch, N. (2012). 4. In *Conversations with God, Book 2* (Expanded ed., pp. 65-68). Charlottesville, VA: Hampton Roads Publishing Company.

we have all bought into without a question at some point in our lives. I began to wonder about whether our beliefs as a collective society were bringing us closer, facilitating harmonious life experiences, or were those beliefs pushing humanity further apart? Christ and Hitler both utilized aspects of group consciousness; they just acted on opposite ends of the spectrum, with different intents and results. Walsch also writes, "Wiping out people is wiping out people, whether at Auschwitz or Wounded Knee." His perspectives make me question what we have learned, and how evolved are the societies of today really, with all of our "rightness" and beliefs?

On an individual basis, our beliefs shape how we perceive and experience the world. Imagine that we see our lives through a picture, and the framing is our beliefs. When we look at a situation, what's revealed in the picture will be the situation, overlaid with supporting aspects of our beliefs, aligning with our personal framing. As your focus is on what you believe to be true, the subconscious mind will automatically eliminate everything else as a possibility, especially anything countering the existing framework of held beliefs. Only the recognizable details within the framework are seen in support of the situation through which you see life.

I had a friend who believed that she always had bad luck and because of her frame of mind, she had a life where she perceived bad things always happened to her. Even when friends pointed out that she had a loving partner, supportive friends and family, and even a great job which she enjoyed and found on her own and by working hard, she still denied that she had a good life and had nothing to be happy about. So that was her experience, jaded by her framing but very real and true to her nonetheless. What you believe is what you will see in your daily life. Like the liquidity of matter, when you believe something, evidence will show up all around you to prove that you are right, especially if you are adamant and unbending in that thinking. You won't even get to notice the alternate options because you are too busy focusing on the very thing you believe to be true and working really hard to make sure it stays true. We will always find and attract examples commensurate with the theory of our notions.

An individual's behavior and thought process may be a result of those societal frameworks and cultural conditioning that the person grew up with. Have you ever stopped, observed and questioned your beliefs? The very ideas you hold about yourself, the people around you, your life experiences and how they may shape the reality around you? After spending several months in Kuwait, I questioned many beliefs that existed within me, wondering if my position on things were blindly accepted truths someone had told me, and whether or not there was any factual basis behind them.

Change can be difficult and apprehension is normal when considering a change in beliefs. Perhaps it is because beliefs act as scaffolding that holds up one's reality. It's comfortable, it's familiar, and who wants to think all this time they've been incorrect? Challenging beliefs can be transformational, healing, and expansive for one person, and very unsettling and disturbing for another. I've always been intrigued by the idea that situations and things in my life aren't fixed, that life and living is more fluid and flexible if we open ourselves to the possibilities. The key is being in a space to allow, while understanding that an answer to a problem or a needed experience will come. Even though the answer may not look exactly like you expected, nor comfortably fit into the framework or in the realm of your beliefs, nevertheless it can still work if we are willing to open and expand ourselves. Through trial and error, my discoveries led me to an understanding that you don't necessarily have to rewire your whole thinking or change every belief to get what you want, you just have to be willing to expand your framing a little at a time. Just by having conscious clarity, curiosity, and openness to a broadened possible outcome, that automatically creates expansion. Beliefs can be changed at any time we chose to change them, just by simply making a new conscious decision to believe something else more positive or empowering.

Other beliefs may be more difficult to change if they are what hold you into a social setting, community, or group consciousness. Religious beliefs are very engrained and oftentimes weaved into cultural interactions and societal rituals, and because of that they could be the most difficult for people to let go of and evolve from. Being born into a Catholic family meant that I grew up participating in many of the Catholic rituals and traditions with family and community around me. Without a contrasting cultural reference, there was nothing to question; this was the way life was. 40 days of Lent (a similar concept to what Muslims do during Ramadan), Palm Sunday, Easter Sunday, Good Friday, midnight mass at Christmas, and confession — that's the way I came into the world. My religious and cultural framing was inherited by what my parents practiced and believed, and that was comfortable and familiar. It wasn't until later in life after leaving the community, that I began to expand my ideas and beliefs, allowing myself to challenge, and question many of my held concepts. None of this would have been possible to do without first, the context of what I came from, and second, the contrast of exposures from other cultures. It has always fascinated me how many different religions and beliefs exist in this world. However you are raised, whatever framework you are born into, it's just one way you can come into the world. Image the hundreds of other ways you could arrive and experience life on this planet, with all the other belief systems.

With all the religious frameworks and ideas about how humans should exist on this planet, they all have similar things in common: they support the idea of a higher source of information to connect with, which leads to an interpretation for how life should be lived. By source, I'm referring to the Higher Power, the Big Man Himself, God, Allah, Great Spirit, or Universe. It's all the same thing, whatever you want to call it. Over the hundreds of years of religions, humans have added and taken away ideas and concepts to these constructs of faith. As diverse as this world may be in the many ways of worship, religions are similar in that they are a source of ethics and faith for many, and can be a source of guilt and fear in many. Each religion has its own set of beliefs and practices for worship. Maybe they are all right and all wrong at the same time. In order to deconstruct this for yourself and further challenge any other held beliefs or societal beliefs in general, you must first ask, what do people gain by holding onto these beliefs and, most importantly, what would they lose if they let go of them? The yardstick used for measuring what's useful to integrate into my life and belief system is a simple question: Do the concepts and insights align with the idea of separateness, guilt, or fear, or do they promote unification, love, and compassion? If it's not the latter, I'm comfortable letting it go.

Take a big picture perspective and see each set of belief systems as a framework or scaffolding. What holds up the scaffolding is the people's participation in the processes that support the existence of these frameworks. Frameworks are important to society because they create order, predictability, and a sense of security for people. The other edge of that sword is that these same structures of beliefs become outdated, and also create limitations for a society or group to evolve. It's like fish in a fish tank. A fish can only grow to a size that can be supported by the environment. Otherwise, the fish would no longer be comfortable or able to survive. A growing plant also needs to be repotted so that its roots have space to expand, looking for nourishment in order to continue its growth. With the root expansion occurring below, there is also expansion and growth simultaneously occurring above, on the surface. The plant might even grow into a large tree, depending on conditions. Society with its belief structures is much the same. How do we continue to evolve and grow, and expand to unrealized potential, if we are not willing to step out beyond the frameworks and scaffolding that lock us into our comfortable positions?

Humans want and need to believe in a reality that they are comfortable with; our known truths. People have forgotten that the access to universal truth lies within each one of us, accessible at any time, based on one's ability to turn inward. I used to believe that people would respond to me in a certain way, and they did. After realizing beliefs held about myself could be changed, ultimately I changed, which in turn changed how people responded to me. Those interactions further strengthened my resolve because evidence was showing up all around me that the more I believed in something new, the more it was presented before me. Sounds like magic, but it's not. It is the cyclical creation of life, which we continuously create by our beliefs as we are having the experience of living. As life is being lived we acknowledge and decipher things that occur, which in turn reinforce our held beliefs. Life responds to us, by concurrently creating us right back with the things we interpret through our framing.

The Universe is a fair friend; whatever you tune into with your beliefs, thoughts, and emotions (beliefs=energy) creates the experience. The good news is that it's possible to change the experience within a reality whenever we change our beliefs. It is a matter of realigning ourselves to something new.

From an energy standpoint, whatever you believe about yourself becomes the resonate energetic signature all around you, and you are constantly vibrating that frequency inward and outward. If you are always telling yourself that you are ill, you will attract more illness and you will be constantly sick. Have you ever met someone who frequently says, "I'm sick, I'm sick, I'm sick?" This person is not only reconfirming the idea to him or herself by dictating to his or her immune system and body on a cellular level how to respond, but now this person is also telling people to witness this constant sickness. Now you have the group consciousness supporting this individual's self-fulfilling prophecy. People around will notice and say, "Yeah, you are sick all the time." People do get sick, but, by and large, illness or wellness is supported with thoughts and emotions. If you are thinking and feeling guilty about that, don't. That's just another belief that you'll have to unravel later. Trust me, don't go there. At the very least, you can begin to look at your emotions and thoughts from a conscious perspective and how they support and align to the situations around you, regardless of whether they are good or bad. If thoughts, beliefs and actions aren't supporting you the way you want, then evaluate what changes can be made to align to something new that will better support your life.

I hear people say all the time that they are open-minded, but as soon as something is presented outside of their existing beliefs framework, they immediately reject what's being said. Try it for yourself. Ask someone if they consider themselves open-minded. Nine times out of ten people will say, "Yes, I'm pretty open-minded." Then, present an idea or rationalization that opposes their current belief and watch them spin like a top. This exercise is not meant to wind people up for no reason, but serves as an example that people often lack self-awareness about how their beliefs cause them to be opposed to new ideas and the possibility of change, and also the idea that things are more fluid than we really understand or may be led to believe. Matt Kahn, a spiritual teacher and author says, "Most people don't see their beliefs. Instead their beliefs tell them what they see. This is a simple difference between clarity and confusion."

My beliefs certainly hindered my own healing process when, for years, I was only willing to look at traditional medicine. Only when I changed my belief system, did I begin to heal at the deepest depths needed.

Beliefs are very personal; this is one of the reasons why most people say it is not polite to talk about religion and politics. I believe that, as a society, we should always push the boundaries of what is acceptable to discuss, to challenge beliefs, and to question the status quo. How else do we evolve and expand as a society if we are not willing to look beyond what is known and comfortable, looking into other potentials and seeing what else might be possible? It's like choosing a more dynamic worldview that's in high definition color instead of just black and white.

CHAPTER 7

New Year in Beirut

"There is nowhere you can be that isn't where you are meant to be."

—The Beatles

Some Lebanese friends of mine working as expats in Kuwait invited me to visit their family house in Lebanon for the New Year's holiday. I was excited to see a new country in the region and had always heard great things about Lebanon.

My friend Joseph had grown up in a small village north of Beirut. I was honored that he invited me to go with him to meet his family and friends. Knowing how concerned my family might be over my traveling to Lebanon, I decided not to tell anyone about my plans until returning to Kuwait. From my perspective, landing halfway across the world and not taking full advantage of chances to see everything possible would be opportunities lost. I wouldn't be able to live with myself having passed up a chance to see Beirut, especially with someone who lived there. It was an amazing experience and Lebanon remains one of my favorite countries. I fell in love with Lebanon's beautiful snowcapped mountains and the intricate winding roads that snaked through, connecting one village to the next. There was limitless nightlife fun, and the social scene was exciting and vibrant. The energy of the people was mesmerizing and inviting; the people of Lebanon are proud and heartfelt about their country.

Joseph picked me up at the airport a couple days before New Year's Eve, and we hopped in his tiny VW, winding through the busy traffic. The city's roads were packed with cars moving in every direction. As we traveled further away from the city, the roads became more winding and narrow. More than once we missed a head-on collision. While I winced at every turn, I could see him smirking as he torqued the engine harder and faster up and around the hills. He was a joker and I knew he enjoyed making me squirm in my seat. The air became clearer the higher we got into the hills, where traffic was also decidedly less. The houses looked old, with their front doorsteps less than a step in from the road. The village itself resembled the set of an old foreign movie. Even in January, the trees were green, while the snow-covered mountains were a breathtaking backdrop to houses perched delicately on the sides of hills. In the opposite direction was the beautiful Mediterranean Sea, the port bustling with ships coming in and out of the harbor.

We finally arrived at the family home. His mother was petite with a kind, sweet smile. His sister was a younger version of her mother, with jet-black hair and big brown eyes. Another gentleman was there, a close dear family friend named Ralph. He was an older Lebanese man with white hair and a big belly. He was a pleasant conversationalist and interested in discussing with me how the rest of the world viewed Lebanon.

Sitting down for dinner, Joseph's mother poured me a much-appreciated glass of red wine and a tall glass of straight scotch over ice for herself. I was slightly shocked to see a Middle Eastern woman drinking hard liquor as a dinner drink, but tried not to display my feelings, turning instead to the dinner conversation. Ralph began by reviewing Lebanon's history, explaining the relationship between Christians and Muslims in Lebanon, as well as how Syria came to occupy certain areas and why the Lebanese were upset by this takeover. He didn't spare the United States, empathically stating that my country had the wrong view of Lebanon, zeroing in on the State Department's website that warned Americans the country was dangerous for travel. He became very emotional, saying that this representation was unfair, focusing too much on Hezbollah as a terrorist organization. Hezbollah, he noted, didn't care about harming the United States or Americans, including me during my stay in the country. What the group did care about was annexing as much land and influence as possible.

Ralph and Joseph's family were of the Christian faith, and their perspectives were ones that were gained by spending their lives wedged between the politics of Muslim and Christian interests within Lebanon and in other parts of that region.

I listened to him without interjecting any of my own comments or opinions, as I knew there was a very long and complex history to the relationships in the region and within Lebanon. His words had a calming effect because there were some concerns about my safety as an American traveling in Lebanon based on what I had read and heard about the actions of Hezbollah. I trusted Joseph and his friends to steer us clear of any danger while we were there. In February, weeks after leaving Lebanon, a car bomb in downtown Beirut killed Lebanon's Prime Minister Rafic Hariri and several of his security detail. In news reports, sources blamed Hezbollah for the bombing, citing the organization's drive for a complete Syrian withdrawal. While Ralph was probably correct that Hezbollah didn't care about Americans in Lebanon, the group's methods were violent and oftentimes innocent people were killed.

Joseph's family was just like he was: hospitable, charming, and fun. They made me feel completely comfortable and welcomed as I settled into their home for my visit. They were curious and inquisitive about my family, life, and culture. They knew a lot about the United States, but they still had many questions.

As we finished dinner, Joseph was excited to show me downtown Beirut, so we set out into the crowded and busy city streets to celebrate a pre-New Year's Eve celebration. I noticed that certain places in the city looked very retro and old, while other buildings were new and architecturally amazing. Since the war, many structures were rebuilt to look modern, while others were partially restored to their original architecture.

In the busy nightlife district, we found a nightclub that was gearing up for the celebration. The party seemed to go on forever, and as one of the guests was opening the door to leave, daylight could be seen just breaking through. How was it possible that we stayed out till dawn? Joseph let me know that bars close in Beirut when the people leave or when the alcohol runs out — whichever comes first. This was the normal nightlife, clubbing scene in Beirut, not just because it was a couple days prior to New Year's Eve. One thing was for sure; in Beirut they knew how to throw a good party.

After recovering from the night's prior festivities, we met some of Joseph's friends at a local café the next day and started off to an Irish pub in the historic part of downtown Beirut. The village was ready for the New Year's Eve celebration. The downtown area was buzzing and full of joy and life, a stark contrast to the machine-gun toting security personnel visible on various street corners. Little white lights strung overhead lit up the cobblestone walkways. Specialty gift shops, cafés, and restaurants lined the streets. Young Syrian boys sold trinkets in the streets. A small Syrian boy carrying a basket of red roses scurried up to our group and rattled something off in Arabic. Joseph told me the boy was trying to sell a rose for me. After inspecting the roses closer we saw that they were not real ones but made of silk. Joseph politely declined but the boy persisted, trailing behind us as we continued walking to the center of the city, finally giving up and finding a new target.

We then focused our attention on the clock tower that marked the center of the city. Joseph explained that during wartime the city had been completely destroyed. What we were looking at was the city completely reconstructed, as it was before the war. When we arrived at the Irish Pub, an older red-headed man with an Irish accent popped out from around the corner and offered us a table in the back of the restaurant where the seven of us could sit. Since mostly Arabic was being spoken, I couldn't follow what was being said. Suddenly one member of our group, Wahid, began speaking to me in English, stating that the U.S. had no right to be in Iraq and that American soldiers were killing innocent people. He muttered a few other things in Arabic and then the entire table fell silent. Everyone was looking at me, waiting for my response.

Seeing the uncomfortable look in Joseph's eyes, I took a gulp of wine, and swallowed it slowly, sensing that I needed to choose my words carefully. Getting into a huge debate would solve nothing, since I could see that Wahid had his mind made up. However, having been a solider, his comments angered me. Still, trying to consider his feelings, I told him that I, too, was unsure if America's continuing presence in Iraq was the right choice. Elected officials, including our president, don't always make the correct choices. While we hoped to bring peace and freedom to Iraq, no one knew whether that could ever happen. Iraq, I said, still had a long road ahead. I told Wahid that the Iraqi people had been deeply hurt and treated inhumanely throughout history and I was sorry for that. But, by disposing Saddam our nation had hoped that the suffering the Iraqis had endured by his hand would stop. Wahid fired back, "But what gives you the right to play the police for the world?" Never expecting to be confronted with such questions, I felt unprepared and caught off-guard. Honestly, the last thing I wanted was to discuss foreign politics or somehow try to explain why my country had done certain things. It was an uncomfortable moment. My response was honest, but admittedly, also a hope to hold off further discussion.

"I don't know how to make heads or tails about being in Iraq, especially in the rest of the world's eyes, and frankly I don't know or care anything about foreign politics," I told him. Since it was the first time anyone from another country had asked me why the United States was there in the Middle East, I realized that there were some other, broader perspectives about America's involvement and that not everyone was happy about it. While not everyone loves America and many were outspoken in their criticisms, the immigration lines to enter the U.S. were not getting any shorter. But this encounter was a wake-up call. I realized that from that time on, wherever I would travel within the Middle East, like it or not, people would see me as representing America, for better or worse.

Joseph interrupted, "Hey guys, let's order food now!" That was his way of breaking the tension and changing the subject. It worked and I was thankful for it. I was still feeling pushed into a corner and a little upset about being confronted so directly about the Iraq situation, somehow making me responsible for my government's actions. From that point on everyone spoke English and the conversation became lighter, however there was still irritation that Wahid had gone there with me.

As the night went on, another person joined us. He approached the table with the smile of a Cheshire cat that reached from ear to ear. He was tall and handsome and was simply stunning to me. I had never met a man who could be described as beautiful, but that description fit this new arrival. He had hazel eyes with a light brown tint and thick curly black hair. When he smiled the light in his eyes danced and his presence lit up the room. He looked into my eyes, said hello, and extended his hand to shake mine. Suddenly, I felt shy, quickly looking away. Quite simply, his presence overwhelmed me. Never in my life had I ever felt shy; my cheeks were getting warm; my face was getting red. I kept wishing that he would just stop looking at me. I was thankful that others at the table had started other conversations and did not seem to notice my red face and nervous wine sipping. As he pulled out the chair and sat directly across from me, Joseph introduced us. His name was Majed.

His English was a little broken, and it took some time for me to understand the way he put his words together. But even that was cute and made me smile even more the longer I listened to him talk. We never took our eyes away from each other and it seemed as though the world around us stopped. There was this instant connection between us, something that was hard to explain. There were periods in the conversation that we just stopped and didn't say anything, but instead of feeling awkward it just felt peaceful. As the night ended we gave Majed and another friend a ride back to their house, which was on the way to Joseph's house. Intrigued by Majed, I didn't want the night to end, I wanted to talk with him more. We exchanged email addresses and said we would keep in touch. He mentioned that he thought he would pass through Kuwait soon, on his way to finding a new contract in Iraq working with the American Army.

Every day and night in Lebanon was a nonstop party, so by the time New Year's Eve came, Joseph and several of his friends decided to ring in the New Year at home with an intimate house party. Friends piled in and the food and alcohol was plentiful. I was content to stay in. After the first couple of nights partying till dawn, the struggle to keep pace with the Lebanese was beginning to take its toll on me. We ate a late dinner around nine o'clock and then socialized and counted down minutes before midnight. Once midnight had passed, the guys decided to go back downtown and hit the club scene. Knowing my limits, I opted out of the continuing festivities and went to sleep.

Waking up to my last day in Lebanon, Majed stopped by where I was staying and we had a chance to say good-bye. He hugged me and looked at me for a moment. It was a meaningful silence; there was a sense of him wanting to say more, but either he couldn't or didn't know how. There was mutual understanding when he looked into my eyes. There was no way that this one meeting was it. We knew that with this connection we had to cross paths again. Although not knowing when or how, I hoped deeply to see him again. Part of me felt silly about falling so hard so fast. How could I meet someone for such a short time and feel so connected to him? But I was unable to resist. I felt like we were magnets, with a force pulling us together. The closer we came to each other, the more intense the pull. We had spent minimal time together but already something between us felt old, familiar, and very nostalgic. His soul felt like that of a very wise man; content, peaceful with some deep wisdom, and knowledgeable about life.

Getting on the plane to journey back to Kuwait, there was a feeling of sadness saying goodbye to Lebanon. I wanted to explore the country more than I did, but time ran out. Deep down, I knew that the probability was high that I would never return, but I would always have the wonderful memories of the time spent there.

CHAPTER 8

Heading North

"Do not follow where the path may lead. Go instead where there is no path and leave a trail."

— Harold R. McAlindon

After journeying back to Kuwait, I settled into things at work, but had trouble getting my head back into the game. I couldn't stop thinking about meeting Majed, about the night we met and the conversations we had. It seemed so silly, for God sakes! I only knew him for a couple of days. I kept thinking, "How could I become so enamored with him? This is crazy!"

Not only was I distracted with thoughts of Majed, but I was bored with my job and the numbing routine of daily activities. Not just the driving gambit to and from work, with the crazy Kuwaiti traffic circles and the mad drivers, but also the long waits to access the base and the routine car checks. My office felt stale and my daily tasks began to feel monotonous and mindless. Certainly, I welcomed the mental distraction of Majed to escape from the monotony.

After a few days I finally received an email from Majed and we started to correspond. I looked forward to reading his emails and hearing about what things he had done that day with his brothers, whether riding motorcycles, taking short road trips, or spending time with his family. He would tell me stories about his father and mother when they were young, and how growing up he had lived all over the Middle East with his family.

Within a few weeks I received news from Majed that he had accepted another contract working in northern Iraq with the U.S. Army. Previously, he worked with contractor security teams and because he spoke Arabic and English, he was also working as an interpreter.

Busy getting back into my life in Kuwait, I had overlooked some of the emails in my inbox. One came from someone I didn't recognize: Mr. Lopez, Network Operations Center, Iraq. While thinking it was strange to be receiving official correspondence from the network operations center in Iraq in my personal email, I quickly understood that it was a job offer to work in Iraq. Weeks earlier, I applied for several positions in Iraq before my tour in Kuwait was completed, never suspecting anything would come through so fast. Before becoming too excited, I called Mr. Lopez directly to confirm the offer. Since the amount of money seemed so high, I thought it might have been a clerical error. After he confirmed the offer, I let him know that the signed contract would be sent over within the next 24 hours. There was no pause, I just said yes.

I arranged to go back to the States in order to get some things taken care of before leaving for Iraq. My mind quickly shot over to the fact that Majed would also be in Iraq. Would we ever have a chance to see each other? My assignment was working within the U.S. Embassy annex supporting the communications backbone for Multi-National Forces Iraq (MNF-I) in the area known as the International Zone. Majed was supposed to be further north in Mosul, so it didn't seem likely our paths would cross. Excited to go, and a little anxious, I began to accept that whatever happened, things would be just fine.

Many people thought I was nuts leaving a perfectly safe job in Kuwait to go to Iraq. It was a little nuts, but I felt drawn to Iraq, like something was pulling me to keep moving. I knew that people were living and working there and that some pockets were better than others. Although a lot of areas in Iraq were active combat zones, I held onto the hope that it couldn't all be as bad as people made it out to be. However, two days before getting on the plane to Iraq, a mortar round hit the U.S. Embassy area where I would be working. The news reported several tragic deaths as a result of the hit. I did pause and reevaluate my decision, but still decided to go. My thought process was, and always has been, hell what's the chance of that happening twice in a row? Besides, whether I'm in Iraq or walking down a lone country road, the Universe will take me when it's my time to go.

On the way to Iraq, I linked up with a couple of guys who would be traveling with me. The first stop on our journey was Fort Benning, Georgia to go through some initial training and to pick up some issued protective gear, such as Kevlar helmets and flack vests, in order to be cleared to travel. We stayed in Georgia for a week, and then flew from Atlanta through Germany, to Kuwait, and finally to Iraq.

At this time, the United States and several coalition partners were only two years into the war in Iraq, initiated by George W. Bush's Global War on Terror (GWOT) mission, which started in the beginning of 2003 with "shock and awe," a controlled air campaign used to overwhelm the opposition with a show of force via airstrikes. Little did we know at the time that "shock and awe" was only the beginning of an eight-year ground conflict that created a governance vacuum and turned the country into a battle ground for extremists from all over the region. Arguably, the intervention left Iraq shakier and more fragmented than ever before. There were over 150,000 American troops in Iraq at the peak of the surge, and over 200 camps, forward operating bases (FOBs) and combat outposts (COPs). MNF-I was the name of the coalition's force taking part in the operation, ironically named "Operation Iraqi Freedom," which was led by the United Kingdom, Poland, Australia, and the United States. I think it is important to point out that America didn't go into this war alone. Many countries stood right alongside, taking part and supporting this operation. North American Treaty Organization (NATO) played a big part with training mission pieces for the Iraqi Army and police forces. NATO is a 28 nation coalition, and in addition to the NATO nations' participation, there were half a dozen more non-NATO coalition partners with a presence in Iraq.

The most difficult part of my trip was the flight from Kuwait to Iraq, flying on an Air Force chartered C-130 from Kuwait to the military side of the Baghdad International Airport (BIAP) in Iraq. As the plane started the descent, circling in a corkscrew pattern known as a combat landing, the erratic up and down movements were nauseating. With the plane bobbing up and down, the pressure in my stomach started building, my throat got tight, my mouth started to water, and my eyes and head were heavy. We would be flying along then suddenly drop several feet and then shoot back up. Then the airplane started this hard banking movement, and with a sudden thud, we were finally on the ground. As I exhaled with relief, a couple of older combat veterans across the aisle chuckled. "It's all in the eyes," one of them told me. "We were taking bets on whether or not you were going to lose those cookies. Way to hang in there!"

A supervisor met us at the U.S. military side of the BIAP and told us we had to hurry to make the connection by helicopter to the international zone. We were hoping not to get bumped by someone else more important. Often times we flew "space A", meaning we could join the flight manifest based on the availability of space after General Officers or other high ranking officials who had the first priority. After loading our gear and bags into the shuttle, we went over to the helicopter pad and were discouraged to learn that the helicopters were grounded for the day because of a sandstorm. Sandstorms often roll in quickly and severely impact visibility, leaving only an orange hazy tint in the air and making it nearly impossible to fly or even drive safely. It was terrible news because it meant sleeping in a temporary housing tent until the helicopters started to fly again. They shuttled us over to the housing coordinator and we got checked in to our tents and sleeping assignments. Walking into the tent I saw two rows of cots and began thinking to myself, here I go again, remembering back to my times in the field at Fort Bragg. I'd come full circle. Having spent more time in the field than I had ever wanted, I had learned a thing or two about sleeping in a tent with a lot of people. First: go as far to the back of the tent as possible because people come in at all hours of the day and night, walking past, making noise. Second: from the back of the tent, you can keep an eye on who is around you, and keep your stuff close and always locked up. Frequently, things will develop legs and walk away.

The all-female tent was mostly clean and empty since there weren't many women around. There were a couple of female soldiers sleeping with their rifles lying beside them. Laying down all my gear and bags under my cot and relocking my suitcase, I grabbed my bath supplies and toothbrush and headed to the shower facility. After traveling for 24 hours, a chance to shower and brush my teeth seemed like a luxury.

To appreciate the shower facilities in those days on Camp Victory base in Iraq you have to understand that you walk, filthy and dirty (sometimes in a sandstorm), about 50 yards to a white trailer building marked "females" on the door. You step into the hot steamy room and wait in line, if there is one. There are eight separate shower stalls, with a flimsy 50-cent shower curtain that never covers the door of the shower or stays closed while you are showering. Every time the door to the trailer opens the shower curtains get pulled and flaps in the wind as you are going about your showering business. You finish the shower, attempt to get dry, and put on clean clothes, meanwhile trying to avoid stepping in the dirt everyone drags in the shower room from outside, which is now mud. It's unavoidable. Despite the obstacles, having a clean body and shampooed hair for the first time in a couple days was better than going without.

Getting my dusty hiking shoes back on and putting my wet hair in a ponytail, I trekked my way back through the sandstorm to the sleeping tent. Sitting on the edge of my cot, wiping the dust off my arms from the walk back in the dirt and grit, it felt like I needed another shower. There was a layer of dirt and dust on everything. Too tired to care, I kicked my shoes off and lay down on the cot. Covering myself with the sleeping bag, I quickly fell asleep. Hours later, I was suddenly woken up by the sound of two people arguing. Judging by the voices, one of them was a male. There was a sign on the door saying that it was explicitly forbidden for males to be in the female tent. The man, a UN worker, was arguing with a female UN worker, speaking a dialect of some African language. Irritated, I walked past them to the reception tent where the house administrative office was and asked for the retired Army sergeant major I had met earlier, who was in charge of the tent city sleeping quarters. After telling him there was a man in our tent yelling at a woman, he jumped out of his chair and was at the door of that women's tent faster than you could say "airborne." He escorted the UN man out of the tent and told him that the base's MPs would arrest him if he ever entered there again. The man tried to deflect the accusations, saying he was a UN representative and had official business with his colleague. The sergeant major sharply retorted, "I don't care if you are the president of the United Nations. You walk in that tent again, I will drag you out personally, and have you arrested by the MPs. You handle your business with your colleagues somewhere else." The man snarled and walked away. The UN woman came to me and thanked me for getting him out of there because he was becoming verbally abusive to her and she was scared of him and what he might do to her physically. But she also warned me that because the man was vindictive, he might find a way to take it out on me later. Everyone clearly knew I made the complaint because I left and then came back with the sergeant major. I reassured her that I would be leaving soon, so there was no worry. I would never see him again. There was no way I would stand by and let the woman be verbally abused by this man, not to mention that it seemed like he was rapidly losing control. How were the rest of the women in the tent supposed to sleep and feel safe with an angry man coming in and out of the tent?

It was getting darker and I still hadn't slept for a solid eight hours because of the travel schedule. Since my short nap had been interrupted I was ready to go back to bed. I noticed that a lady had come in while I was asleep and was in the cot next to mine. She was an older woman, in her early 60's from upstate New York; she was a journalist writing a story about women in combat in Iraq. She piped in and said, "You got some moxie kiddo." "Yea?" I replied, "Moxie is the name of that terrible tasting soda we had growing up in Maine." She laughed, "Yes, I've heard of that drink. It's an acquired taste isn't it? I think you can still buy it." She added, "I knew you were a Yankee as soon as you started talking." She extended her hand and said, "My name is Gloria." I shook her hand. "I'm Darcy; what does that mean, to have moxie?" She said, "You know someone who has the chops to question things and act in difficult situations, not letting things slide by as is." I responded, "I guess I do have moxie."

Soon after, I drifted off to sleep. It was an early morning wake-up with the sound of people rustling around in the tent, preparing to move on to whatever places they were destined to go. Gloria and I said good-bye and wished each other luck. She was heading north and still had one more night in tent city before she could catch her ride. There were still some pretty "hot" places in the north, with pockets of heavy bombing and frequent reports of enemy sniper activity. I was impressed by her courage to travel to Iraq. This didn't seem like a place someone in her 60's would want to hang out in, but hey, I suppose, that's proof that it's never late to start a new journey.

The part of Victory Base we stayed in was a transitional area with temporary housing for people entering and leaving Iraq. I was happy to finally be moving on to my final destination, the International Zone (IZ). We managed to jump on an early helicopter and took the 30-minute ride to the helicopter pad in the IZ. I was ready to stop dragging my bags across the world and finally land somewhere.

My brain was feeling a bit foggy, and I hadn't caught up on my sleep from the days of travel. After landing, we were picked up by the company management team. They brought us to the compound where we would stay and assigned us to our rooms. The compound was an old textile building and all the offices were converted into rooms for the employees. They were small, but private rooms with a shared bathroom and shower. It was nice to finally reach a place where I could unpack and settle in for the time being. I was antsy to check my email and send a note to my family and Majed to let them know of my safe arrival. A couple days before I made it to Iraq, there was another explosion at a green zone café where a lot of Americans and other expats hung out, socializing over food and drinks after work. Most of these incidents made the evening news and I wanted to let my family know that everything was fine. Knowing my family, they would really be watching the news now for anything happening in the IZ in Iraq.

After getting my computer hooked-up and the Internet working, I sent a couple of quick notes home. There was one email from Majed, checking in to see where I was. He was still in Lebanon trying to get money for the flight to Iraq. The company was expecting him to find his own transportation to Iraq. What cheapskates, I thought! They could never pull that on an American. So far, the only communication we had was by email. I was anxious to see him again in person. In his email, he also wrote that he was watching "too much" American movies so his English would improve. He said that he hoped I was doing fine and wished that he could see me again someday. There was a smile on my face while drafting a quick note back to him, asking what movies he had been watching and letting him know I wished him a safe journey soon to Iraq.

At the end of the 12-14 hour workdays, which were six and mostly seven days a week, a few of us started sitting on the rooftop of the building where we lived. The building looked slightly war-torn, with the disparate bullet holes from previous year's "shock and awe" strewn across the walls. We found beer and wine at local *bakalah* shops in the IZ and would sit on the roof, out of the sight of others, and attempt to wind down and escape for a few moments of solitude.

I was already starting to imagine coming back to the U.S., not having to wear a bulletproof vest and helmet to work every day. I was thankful to not be under the constraints of the uniformed personnel. They were under stricter uniform mandates and they couldn't leave at will. Nonetheless, the contractor routine had already started to wear on me. It was hot, sweaty, and heavy to carry the gear from one place to another, most of the time walking, and so after a while I just stopped wearing it. A lot of other contractors who had been there for a long time stopped wearing it as well. After a period of time, complacency starts to set in. Sitting on the rooftop of our building, we could hear machine guns firing and bombs going off in the distance. It was surreal to hear this combat happening while we sat there listening. To think that, less than a mile away from the walls of the compound where we resided, a battle was raging. The thought felt heavy and grim. There were days when it was very sobering and surreal to be there.

Often I would sit in the network operations center (NOC), seeing the reports come in about bombs and explosions going off around the various parts of the country. Some days there were legitimate explosions from terrorist groups and the media would quickly grab it and within minutes they were off and running with the story. One day, I watched a helicopter malfunction and crash within my sightline, as a nearby monitor in the NOC played out the footage in real-time on its 24-hour feed. The crash was fatal for the multi-national coalition forces personnel inside of it. As smoke rolled out from the top of the rotor, the helicopter started leaning to one side and quickly descended before crashing into the ground. The media swiftly reported on the story as a terrorist attack, and, without hesitation, terrorist groups claimed credit for the crash. A quick one-liner across the bottom of the T.V. monitor eventually clarified that the crash was actually a mechanical malfunction, and the media was off and running onto the next biggest story. Of course, in those days, because of the chaos, the stories were fast and furious with regular attacks and explosions happening, but there were plenty of events that were untold, exaggerated, or just reported incorrectly. I believe this contributed to the fear and misunderstandings of those watching the events unfold outside of the country.

After several weeks, I decided to take a day off to travel along with a colleague to some other sites. I'd only been in the country for a short time and was already antsy to see something else. That day we managed to get manifested for a helicopter going to Camp Victory with some international coalition soldiers. Getting situated and buckling myself into the Blackhawk, I started to have thoughts of rocket-propelled grenades (RPG's) and random gunfire. Taking inventory, I had second thoughts about whether to go. My travel partner assured me that the helicopter's route to Victory was relatively safe and secure. That reassurance wasn't much when someone uses the word "relatively" while describing safety in a combat zone, but it was enough to keep me on the chopper.

The helicopter's take-off was quick, an energetic leap into the sky, with a quick swoop to the right and then back to the left. We quickly got up to our cruising altitude. Looking down at what seemed like merely a couple hundred feet above the ground, I noticed how the helicopter tethered back and forth. Initially, I thought the pilot was giving us a guided tour of Baghdad, but really he was just trying to avoid random gunfire from some of the rooftops and keep us from getting shot down through a rough patch of the city. Further along, I was amazed to see the activity of the people below and how they had become accustomed to the sound and shadows of helicopters passing over them and their concrete and marble homes. Passing over neighborhoods and the uneven grid of closely intertwined streets, I thought of a familiar neighborhood near where I grew up.

Looking intently out the window, I was trying to see anything exciting going on, like maybe a gun fight or some shadow of the eerie Baghdad as portrayed by CNN, which I witnessed in the safety of my Kuwaiti living room months before. I saw nothing. There was only a beautiful afternoon with young Iraqi children playing soccer in a small patch of a lush grassy field, surrounded by buildings and a half-mangled chain fence.

The tall date palm branches swayed back and forth in the breeze that was generated by the helicopter's colossal blade rapidly chopping through the air. I tried to imagine what it was like for the people living here as they strolled and biked through streets lined with former homes and businesses that were now bombed-out structures riddled with bullet holes. From above, I noticed that many of these homes utilized their flat rooftops for storage, leisure space, and a place to hang laundry. On the rooftops across Baghdad, there were many satellite dishes for television.

In the distance, I noticed a large concrete building, surrounded by cranes and tall structures that reminded me of the minarets of a mosque. My travel partner thought that it was another palace of Saddam's whose construction had been interrupted by the start of the war. To me it looked out of place; a monstrosity of a castle in the midst of a bunch of tiny modest village homes.

As we descended to our landing on the Hilo pad at Camp Victory Base, my heart fluttered. We touched down with a heavy thud. I could hear the rotors of the helicopter slowing down and stopping as the doors flew open. We were once again greeted by our crew chief as he hopped off while extending his hand to help me down. "Have a nice day, ma'am and thank you for flying the friendly Baghdad skies with U.S. Army airways!" Giving him a quick sarcastic grin, I grabbed his arm for stability while hopping down to the ground. I laughed, appreciating his effort to lighten his day.

We walked along the flight line and toward the flight manifest office. Our immediate priority was to find a way back to the IZ that day. The flights between Camp Victory, IZ, and the other FOBs filled up fast and if the flights were all booked, we would find it difficult convincing some General to allow us to fly with him and his staff. Failing that, our options would be to take the Rhino bus, an up-armored shuttle transport, usually with an armed convoy and running at very high speeds. Because of roadside bombs, that ride would be dangerous and nerve-wracking. Our last resort was to enjoy a night in the luxurious tent city, with the hope of making a morning flight.

We walked for about 20 minutes, wearing our bulletproof vests and helmets (required to have when flying); I was starting to reminisce back to my Army days, never thinking that after leaving the military I would be here doing the things I was doing, especially in Iraq.

131

Our next stop was the Army dining facility (DFAC). As always, I wanted to enter and leave as quickly as possible, trying not to be noticed or draw attention to myself. Since I was one of few women living amongst GI's, who had not seen many women for a long time, that mission was always nearly impossible. I got through it fairly easily because I had a male coworker with me. He knew how to manage the blocking and deflecting of the advances, allowing me to detour away from the advances of random conversations and small talk.

I had never been to this base and was interested to get a tour of Al-Faw Palace, which was a little newer and even more brilliant than the main palace in the IZ. The Victory Palace had light-colored floors and marble pillars that extended up to the 20-or-30-foot ceiling. The intricate chandeliers, apparently handmade, were laid with crystals that were stacked methodically, with layers spiraling around and creating an amazing display of craftsmanship. Winding staircases led to various rooms that were turned into cubicle farms now occupied by the Army and different government agencies and departments. As I walked through, I couldn't prevent my mouth from falling open with awe. The detail and design that had been put into the marble work and layout of this building was the most extraordinary thing I had ever seen. There were colors and types of marble that I never even knew existed.

My coworker Jon, who traveled there with me, borrowed a vehicle and a driver for the day so we could more easily move around the base. The driver announced that he was taking us someplace that would be a surprise to see. He rolled up to a stop at the end of a long direct driveway and

132

told us to look to the right. "See the small building there?" he asked. "That's where they are keeping Saddam in prison until the trial." Though I didn't know if he was telling us the truth or passing along a rumor, just the thought that Saddam might be that close sent chills down my spine. I was silent for a moment as I thought about how Iraq's former dictator might be living, what the conditions were for him in prison.

People quickly learned one important fact about Camp Victory—it had the best PX shopping in the country. The rule of thumb while deployed is if you see something you think you want or need in the PX, you never wait. You buy it immediately because you never know when it will be there again, if ever. Even in February the PX was crowded with people running all over the place, reminiscent of Christmas shopping season in the States. Everyone seemed to know what they wanted to buy but me. Impressed with the warehouse-like shelves stocked with goods up to the ceiling, I turned a corner while looking up and suddenly found myself swept off my feet by someone rushing around the corner. Sitting on the ground, I looked up, stunned at the person who was standing in front of me. "Majed?" I said. "Oh My God," he said. "You are here! I am so happy to see you! I knew I might run into you, but not like this."

He reached down, picked me up off the ground, hugged me and kissed my forehead, apologizing over and over again for knocking me over. I was speechless and in shock to see him. We hadn't had contact in over a week and he had expressed a great deal of uncertainty about when he would actually be in Iraq. So the collision was really unexpected, in more ways than one.

We had some time before we needed to catch our flight back to the IZ so we sat outside and had lunch, and he waved off his friends that were waiting for him. While we ate, he told me about his journey to Iraq from Lebanon, how he ran out of money paying off his father's debts and was then unable to afford a plane ticket. Not to be deterred, he spent three days hitchhiking and taking buses from Lebanon through Syria. When he reached Iraq, he hired a taxi driver to take him to the Baghdad International Airport (BIAP), and then he walked the rest of the way. While, to me, what he did sounded insane and even dangerous, I figured as he was a native to the region, what he did probably wasn't that big of a deal.

Jon was getting nervous about missing the flight. We had to get back to the IZ, but I wanted to figure out how to see Majed again. We went over the complicated logistics that would be involved with seeing each other, since he would live on Camp Slayer on the other side of Camp Victory. I told him how to get himself manifested for a helicopter flight and how to plan travel back and forth with the Rhino buses if needed. We spent our last moments saying good-bye, and before I knew it, Jon and I were back on the helicopter.

By now, it was dusk and with the loss of daylight we could see the tracer rounds leaving the machine guns as the soldiers fired through the air every so often, deterring any potential attackers from taking potshots at us that could result in our chopper being shot down. Happy to touch down without incident once again, we headed back to our compound to get ready for the following workday.

Under usual circumstances, I would walk or ride a bicycle the six blocks from the compound where we lived to where we worked in signal annex, located inside the embassy compound. Making the morning commute by foot, seeing the Humvees carrying armed soldiers on the streets passing me by, I often thought about how life might have been in Baghdad before the troops arrived. Once at the embassy annex, I walked through the security checkpoint located on the side that led directly into the dining facility so that I could grab a banana or a piece of fruit before heading into my office.

My routine and level of workload varied from day to day. Sometimes I had a phone in each hand, plus a cell phone ringing on my desk, and emails jamming my inbox, network alarms going off indicating hits to the communication assets, and reports and updates that had to be generated and sent almost hourly. Total chaos. Everything was urgent, with spot reports and briefings needing to be prepared with very little notice, depending on the war events of the day in Iraq. At other times, I watched the minutes slowly tick by, waiting for the day to end so that I could check off one day closer to seeing Majed. Occasionally, Majed would call me as I walked back to the living quarters compound and we would talk about our day. He would ask me about English words or phrases that he didn't understand. I noticed that his English was getting much better each day. It seemed that his dedication to watching American movies and working with Americans was starting to pay off.

Thursday night was a party night in the IZ. Actually, there was something going on nearly every night in the IZ, either a get-together or small party with plenty of alcohol and music so that people could blow off steam and/or make fools of themselves. The favorite places to gather on various nights included the FBI compound, the Adnan Palace (which had a DJ, a small dance floor, and a bar), the PCO compound near the combat support hospital (CSH, pronounced "cash"), the Army special agents' villa, the South African villa, the Italian villa, the British Ministry of Defense (MOD) house, the Special Forces (SF) compound, and probably a few I'm leaving out. There was never a dull moment or a night where people weren't gathering, finding ways to pass the time or trying to make the best of their time in Iraq.

Friday nights became the night that Majed would most often visit the IZ. He showed up later in the evening, usually after ten o'clock at night, and then he left late afternoon the next day. Very few people, if anyone, ever saw or noticed him. I liked that because that meant no one was in my business and it allowed me some semblance of privacy.

Friday nights were late nights for me as I waited for him to come in. Usually he arrived on the Rhino bus since the bus stop was a couple blocks from the living quarters. Our routine never seemed to vary. When he saw me, he would grab me, hug me, and spin me around, lifting my feet from the ground. He would do this funny thing that I quickly named his "greeting." He would kiss me on the forehead, then the nose, left cheek, right cheek, lift my face and kiss my neck, then my lips. I'm not sure how it started but he did it all the time and it was something I always looked forward to when we reunited.

Most of our time together was spent talking, laughing, and asking a lot of questions about each other's families and cultures. One day, he told me about a girl that his family wanted him to marry in Australia. As he spoke, there was an ache in the pit of my stomach at the thought of him going there and marrying someone else. I asked him what he thought he should do and he told me that he wanted to be with a woman that he knew and truly loved, not with someone forced on him by his family. He said that he wanted to do what made him happy, and then added that spending time with me made him happy. Hearing him say that made me happy as well.

While Majed resisted his parents' attempts to arrange a marriage, he told me that at one time, he thought about marrying a woman he didn't know after hearing about her situation on TV. The woman, in her early teens, was from a small village in Afghanistan. After the Taliban raided her village, she was taken from her home, raped, and then left behind to face her family. As a result, her brother and father called her a shame to the family and beat her. She was considered damaged goods, could no longer be married off, and was perceived to be a burden to the family. Majed told me that he had tears in his eyes while watching this story on TV. "At the time, I felt like going to Afghanistan and kicking both her father and brother's asses and then marrying this girl. This makes me angry how they are treating women in these places and I really feel so much sadness when I see this." He was a man of pure heart, and seeing these types of grave injustices to women deeply disturbed him, which he vocalized without restraint.

One Thursday evening, Majed showed up unexpectedly at the living quarters compound. I was surprised because he had told me that the Rhino buses weren't running because of imminent danger from roadside bombs from BIAP to IZ. On that day, there had been multiple roadside bombs, so as a precaution, the busses weren't doing their normal runs. At three a.m. there was an unexpected knock at my door. I was sleepy-eyed and irritated, but I answered the door anyway and found Majed standing there, his khaki pants, black shirt, and backpack covered in dust and holding a long stem red rose. I was shocked to see him. I had no idea how he managed to make it to my living quarters and find a long stem red rose along the way.

"How did you get here?" I asked. He explained that he took a chauffeur. I couldn't understand what he meant and continued to ask him questions. Finally I said, "You mean you hired a TAXI! You took a taxi to get here?!" "Yes, riding in a car, by a chauffeur, from the BIAP through the red zone into the green zone in a taxi." He said all this calmly as he sat on my bed, started to unlace his boots, and get undressed. Upset at his reckless behavior, I begged him to please never do something like that again. "Please, it's too dangerous!" During this time period in Iraq, there could be anywhere from 10 to 15 car bombs a day in any region of the country. Americans soldiers named the main road from the BIAP to IZ Route "Irish," maybe because anyone who made it to the end without being hit by a car bomb must have had "the luck of the Irish" with them.

He told me, "I don't care. It's worth it to see you. Please don't worry about me because you know only the good die young, and I am Majed: bad to the bone!" He told me this with a deeply serious voice, smiling and flexing his biceps. He knew that I would never stay upset with him for very long. We both started laughing and he started tickling me. "Do you make fun of me now?" he asked. While I was still a little upset that he did that, secretly I was glad to see him and loved that he was there. He often joked and said that he was bad to the bone, but on the inside I didn't see that part of him at all, ever. All I could see was a good-hearted man.

We would sleep next to each other, dozing off-and-on throughout the day, making love, talking, and sometimes venturing outside for food. Mostly, we couldn't be bothered with getting dressed and being out in the hot sun. We wanted to lie next to each other and talk. Sometimes we would just be with each other and say nothing for a long time. There were even times we would look at each other and just start laughing for no reason, like giggling children in a fit of laughter.

We discussed religion. I had a lot of questions about what he believed. It was interesting to me that he was there helping the U.S., which was not without great risk to himself or his family. He told me his thoughts on what happened with the Muslim extremists in Iraq and in other parts of the Middle East. He expressed his disagreement and displeasure with what Islamic extremists were doing in the name of religion and how he felt their behaviors and actions reflected poorly on everyone else who was Muslim.

We talked about non-physical, metaphysical, spiritual, and magical things. We always talked about our dreams. As soon as we woke up we would tell each other about what we saw and felt. He told me that he believed in prophecy and that people could come to us and we could see prophetic things in our dreams and visions that would have meaning if we took the time to understand them. He told me stories from the Koran about a man who was held in high esteem by a king because he had the gift of prophecy through his dreams. Majed always spoke humbly about what he thought he knew, and always qualified his opinions by adding that, "Of course we can't know everything."

While his English was getting better, his vocabulary was still limited and at times, there wasn't much "fluff" in the conversations. His words were simple and to the point. I think this is part of the reason the relationship grew so fast and we bonded so quickly, because there was nothing extraneous to decipher between us.

The next morning after Majed's surprise, I opened my eyes and saw the red rose on my nightstand. The night before wasn't a dream. But when I rolled over, he wasn't there. Turning quickly, I looked around the room for anything that might belong to him, proving he was still there. Finally, spying his backpack on the edge of the bed, I relaxed. Leaning back on my pillow, I inhaled and caught a hint of his cologne. It was sweet and permeated the pillowcase. I turned my face into the pillow, breathing in his scent longer.

My bedroom door slowly opened and I closed my eyes and pretended to be sleep. He was quietly moving around, but I heard his clothes fall to the floor. He crawled into bed behind me burying his face in my hair and squeezing me tightly. "Are you awake?" he asked softly. "Yes," I said, rolling over to face him. He looked at me and said: "I love you; do you want to marry me?" Frozen and completely shocked I replied, "You want to marry me?" "Yes, of course. I love you," he stated matter-of-factly.

My mind was turning quickly. "What about the United States? What are we going to do? How can that work? We won't work and live in Iraq forever." He said, "I don't care where we live or what we do. I don't care how far away you are. We can always be together, no matter what. We can always be together if we want to." I said, "Yes, yes we can, but we need to wait." This was a familiar road that had been traveled before and I was not sure it was wise for me to do it again. At the same time, I couldn't deny that the way I felt with him was like nothing I had ever felt before.

Still, I was not blind to the fact that life, love, and marriage in a war zone is quite different from how it is in the real world. Over the years, I had seen how unlikely connections and bonds could be easily built when people found themselves in extreme conditions. Most of the time, these relationships fell apart once this extreme environment was left behind.

There was no question that I cared deeply for Majed, who I considered my soul mate. However, I wasn't confident that we would be able to create a semblance of a life together in the real world. There was a nagging feeling that there wasn't a forever in this scenario for me and Majed.

CHAPTER 9

Soul Reunion

"Every individual soul chooses the significant people in that life. Destiny will place you in the particular circumstance: it will dictate that you encounter a particular person, at a certain time, place."
— Brian Weiss

We had only been in Iraq for five months, but it seemed like I had been there for an eternity. We had been working long days and both Majed and I were ready for a vacation. For our holiday, we decided to go to Jordan to visit the Dead Sea. It was an easy decision because the flight to Jordan from Baghdad International Airport via C-130 (military transport aircraft), courtesy of the US Air Force, was direct, easy, and free.

I had always wanted to visit the Dead Sea and Petra, a historic city in southern Jordan that had been featured in the film, *Indiana Jones and the Last Crusade*. The flight from BIAP to Amman was about 55 minutes. Majed arrived before I did and took a detour to Kuwait so that he could open a bank account. He had been carrying around his salary in cash for the last several months. He flew directly into Amman and I arrived later in the evening, around nine o'clock. I was on edge, worried that the flight would be cancelled and I wouldn't make it to Amman in time for our rendezvous. My flight was delayed several hours due to a sand storm. While frustrating, it was business as usual when flying out of BIAP.

After my plane landed, I made it to the airport lobby and saw Majed waiting for me and holding a taxi outside. He had an ecstatic look on his face and was smiling from ear to ear. He grabbed me and gave me "the greeting." It had been almost two weeks since we had seen each other. His arms felt good around me and his chest was warm and invited me in for a while. As we started making our way to the taxi, he was excitedly talking about all the things that were at the resort we had chosen. He had checked in earlier in the day and had done some exploring. The cab ride to the resort was about 30 minutes; the traffic was heavy, but a bit more civilized than the Kuwait traffic that I knew so well.

We arrived at the resort in the evening just after dark. The staged lighting around the gardens and plants on the hotel grounds, not to mention the amazing view overlooking the Dead Sea, made it look like an oasis. Majed led me to the room we'd call home for the next ten days, located down a winding path that was made from stone and stucco buildings. There was a beautiful fountain in the center where all the paths converged, with amazing date palms and red and pink flowers growing alongside. It felt like our own personal paradise.

On our balcony was a small café table and plush couches. We sat to enjoy the deep blue haze on the horizon of the Dead Sea, the West Bank and Israel. We sat outside watching the sunset, enjoying the fresh and quiet Jordanian night. On our second night there, however, we were startled by sudden bangs and explosions going off just to the right of the buildings next to us. Majed grabbed me and pulled me to the floor of the balcony, under the table. Not moving, we listened as a few more explosions went off, with light crackling after the bang. "Wait a second," I said, poking my head up, "That sounds familiar." I saw some beautiful colors across the sky. We realized that it was just fireworks going off for a celebration beside our building. We began laughing hysterically, still on the floor of the balcony. After spending time in Iraq, it was clear that we had to get used to peace, and maybe learn to forget the explosions for a while.

The next day, we rented a chauffeured car to take us from Amman to Petra so that we could explore some ancient and famous landmarks. Halfway to Petra, we were stopped at a checkpoint on a narrow road with rocks and hills on both sides. Three Jordanian police asked us to get out of the car while they searched it. They were speaking Arabic and I could only pick up a few words here and there. Majed whispered to me in English, explaining that they were doing a routine check and he reassured me not to worry. I noticed that one of the police officers standing off to the side of the road was staring at us as he chain-smoked cigarettes right down to the filter, lighting each one off the last one. He said something in Arabic to his friend and then his friend said something to Majed and our driver.

Majed turned to me and said they were asking to see our passports. He started speaking to them in Arabic, and I started to feel nervous about how they were talking to each other. I could feel the tension and inflections in their voices and the men on both sides started to stand a little taller as if they were posturing toward each other. I told Majed to tell him our passports were in the safe in the hotel. He motioned to me to not talk, and as soon as he did the chain-smoking man said something that sounded like he was asking if I was an American. "Yes, I'm American," I said in English. With big smiles on their faces, the three men changed their demeanor and began shaking my hand and greeting me to their country in English. The men looked at Majed and asked if we would come into their roadside hut to have tea with them. He told them that we were already late on our travel plans and really needed to get going. The men understood and let us go, waving and saying good-bye to me in English as we drove away. Majed said he was hesitant to tell them I was American because he wasn't sure if they were going to start trouble. He asked me why I said something. I wasn't really able to explain what I did. There was a sense within me that in that moment everything was going to be fine. More times than not in my travels, especially in the Middle East, being American has never caused me any trouble. Rather, like with those policemen, being an American has afforded me some lucky breaks.

Petra was beautiful, with tall, sand-colored rock formations, and reddish clay dirt against deep blue skies. It reminded me of places in the Western United States. We decided to take a guided horse tour to ride through, and our two tour guides pointed out landmarks and buildings

145

that were carved into rock formations. Majed had never been on a horse and he was sliding from side to side in the saddle, trying to maintain his balance while also operating the reins. Towards the end of the trail ride, he got the hang of things, and we began to trot back. Our tour guides, nervous about us getting too far ahead of them, began jogging beside us up the trail. They started to yell for us to hold back. Majed looked at me with a mischievous grin and went a little faster. Then, of course, I went a little faster to keep up. Then he went faster to get ahead of me, and before we knew it, we were in an all-out sprint, racing each other up the dirt trail back to the stables.

The horses did not have to be coerced; as soon as they figured out that they were heading back to the barn, they were fully on board with going as fast as their legs would carry them. We sprinted on horseback back up the long dirt road, weaving between screaming tourists. Funnily enough, groups of Asian tourists seemed oblivious to our intrusion, taking pictures around us as we pressed forward toward the barn. Trailing behind were the Jordanian tour guides, galloping as fast as possible, chasing us while screaming, "Stop! Stop! Horse thieves!!" When we finally reached the barns, the horses were breathing heavily and so were we from all the excitement and laughing. The elderly man in charge of the stable began scolding us in Arabic and Majed apologized, claiming it was his first time on a horse and he was not able to control how fast it ran. Majed also praised the man for having such fine and strong horses, comments which seemed to defuse the confrontation long enough for us to slide away. We found our driver and he took us to a small Lebanese diner for lunch and hookah, and then we headed back to Amman.

The rest of our days in Amman were spent sun bathing by the pool or by the Dead Sea, making love, listening to music, spending time in the spa, eating wonderful food, and drinking fruity drinks with umbrellas in them. Before we knew, our vacation was coming to an end and we had to get back to Baghdad.

Our last night in Amman, we talked about a future in which I would meet his family, we would get married, and he would eventually move to the U.S. The timeline was uncertain. We both wanted to stay in our jobs a bit longer in order to save money for the obstacles that might arise due to our being together. Each time we talked, emotions welled up inside of me because our time together in Amman felt like a dream and I didn't want to wake up. Looming just around the corner was the reality of very long workdays and more seven-day workweeks since one of our team members had quit just before I had left for the vacation. All this was waiting for me at the end of that C130 ride into Baghdad. It would be more difficult for us to figure out how to see each other now that we were working this insane schedule.

We landed in BIAP and said our tearful good-byes, with a long hug and kisses. Getting back to the IZ from BIAP at midnight was a quick Rhino ride, and one of my colleagues picked me up from the bus stop and brought me back to our compound.

As I unpacked and pulled the sand-covered clothes from my bag, the scent of suntan lotion lingered on my bathing suit and I started to remember the days we had just spent together. Thoughts began creeping in about whether my

147

current job was worth it if I couldn't be with the one I loved. Was the money I was earning worth sacrificing my life, our time together, and building a future life in the U.S.? How long could I go on working like this, away from my daughter and family? In those days, working as a contractor in Iraq meant good money, more than I had ever made in my life, but the hours and stress that came with it made me question the reason I was still there.

Weeks went by and I started to feel less and less ok with being in Iraq. It seemed like Groundhog Day. I dealt with the same situations and the same people every day, even food began tasting the same. I was becoming increasingly unhappy, partly because of my exhaustion with the operational tempo, and partly because I was sick and tired of dragging Kevlar vests and helmets everywhere we went. The long stressful hours with no days off were wearing me thin and our incompatible schedules meant I hadn't seen Majed since we got back from our vacation. My growing level of frustration meant my days in Iraq were numbered. My search for jobs back in the States began. Majed agreed that it was probably best that we both leave. I would go back first to the U.S. to set something up, and then we could meet up in Beirut later.

After a few weeks my notice was given and, a month or so later, I left Iraq. As a result of a clerical error, I ended up with a two-week stopover in Kuwait while waiting for my exit flight to be coordinated by my company. I wasn't upset because Majed was able to meet me and we spent time in Kuwait together while waiting for my flights to be arranged.

On the day of my flight back to the States, Majed brought me to the airport. He walked me as far as he could and we said our goodbyes again. He held my head in his hands and said, "This is the last time we say good-bye like this. We see each other again in a few months, and then no more time apart." I really wanted to believe him but something inside of me felt sadder than any other time we had ever said good-bye. There was an unsettled feeling that I would never see him again. Walking down the gangway to the plane, my eyes filled with tears, my chest felt tight, and my heart pounded. Each step I took pulled me further away from him. Once in my seat, I put on my headphones and tried to compose myself for the long flight home.

Months went by. I was living and working back in North Carolina. Majed and I were in contact with each other as he was getting ready to leave Iraq for Lebanon so we could meet up again. He could always sense my restlessness with the distance between us. He knew that I wanted him to depart Iraq and was in fear about him still being there. Whenever I tried to raise the issue, he would say, "I'd rather live one day as a lion than an eternity as a sheep." Being with him would be interesting because he was always seeking out adventures that would allow him to live life to the fullest. I admired, loved, and understood that desire about him, because I related to his passion for living life and never wanted to interfere with him doing things he loved. I did, however, feel a growing concern about how our lives would come together. We both wanted to live life's great adventures, and we wanted to live together, but the question was, how? Our cultures, backgrounds, and career paths were worlds apart. The blending and balancing of our lives together never felt like it would really happen and that created much sadness within me.

We talked about plans for me to travel to reconnect with him and meet his family. With just days away from finalizing our travel arrangements, my worst fears came true. Majed was back in Lebanon, riding his motorcycle around a dangerous corner on a dark and rainy day, when he collided head-on with a car. He died of severe head injuries hours after the crash, barely reaching the hospital. It was surreal. 12 hours earlier, we had talked on the phone, and now he was dead. Since I was thousands of miles away, I did not learn about his death until he was already buried. His brother was the one to break the news to me, calling me on instant messenger. *"Darcy, I'm the brother of Majed. I'm sorry to tell you Darcy, Majed has died. He crashed on his motorcycle."* I heard what he said, but did not believe him. The news was so sudden that I was in complete denial. I quickly sent an email to Majed, hoping it was a bad joke or a mistake. Shocked and confused, I began running possible scenarios through my mind. Maybe something happened or changed and he didn't want to see me. I just spoke to him hours ago; he was looking forward to seeing me, we have plans, this cannot be true, why would he do this?

As the awful truth began to sink in, it felt like the worst punch in the stomach, the kind that hurts more if you take a deep breath. I was in shock and did not know what to do next; I just kept staring at my already-packed suitcase. My mother watched the whole thing unfold, from the moment that I received the news. In an effort to be supportive, she started hovering. But the attention was just too much for me; I needed quiet and solitude. I would sit in my room with my door closed and my mind racing, trying to make sense of this tragedy. How could this have happened? Why? With my mom, who was obviously worried incessantly knocking on my bedroom door and asking me questions that were unanswerable, I needed to get away. Jumping in my car, I went to 7-Eleven and bought a pack of cigarettes. I hadn't smoked in years, but I smoked the whole pack. I needed something. My hands were shaking so badly that I could barely light each cigarette. My mind started flashing back through all the moments that we had shared, the things he said to me, and the promises he made. I began to remember things he said that may have presaged his death, that only the good die young, that he never saw himself old, that he didn't want to live like an old man with someone else feeding him and wiping his butt for him in his senior years. I was angry with him for his reckless behavior on his motorcycle, which I had begged him to sell. He knew all along that he wouldn't live to be old and yet he took such big risks.

My friend Jenn heard the news from my mother and began calling me. They were concerned and asked a lot of questions, but I found it hard to tell them the story. It was hard to discuss something that didn't seem real or make any sense to me. Not wanting to talk or cry, I just needed everyone to be quiet and let me process things. I would cry soon though, and a lot.

Days later, the full meaning of the news was still sinking in while daily life continued to swirl around me. As more days passed by, however, the shock wore off and my emotions caught up with me. Several days were spent in bed and I don't remember much about that time. I know that I got up to use the bathroom, drink some water, eat a bite of something, and then crawl back into bed and shut my eyes. Feeling destroyed emotionally, I didn't know what to do next. We had been moving forward on a journey together and now everything had come to an abrupt halt. My life felt lost, and there was agony over the fact that I would never hear his voice, or feel his arms around me again. I felt like my heart was ripped straight out of my chest, there was this gaping hole, and my soul was never going to recover from the loss. I was drowning in the grief of losing my soul mate.

One afternoon after finally getting out of bed, my mom convinced me to get some fresh air and sun for a while by the pool. It was nice to be out, but after an hour or so there was this sudden and overwhelming tiredness, and I could barely keep my eyes open. Going back inside, and laying down for a nap, I went into a deep sleep where a dream unfolded. I walked into this beautiful room filled with a soft white light. Majed was lounging on big, white, feather bed pillows. He was rolling around, smiling and enjoying the comfort he felt all around him. I immediately noticed the feeling of love and warmth in this place, and how bright and soft he looked. He sat on the edge of the bed and I placed my head in his lap. While he stroked my hair away from my face, tears rolled down my cheeks and I told him of my sadness that he was gone. I told him it was hard to see how my life would go on or how I could ever stop feeling this great loss and pain. He said, "*Habibti*, I'm fine and so happy. It's a wonderful place and nice here. I'm really happy." I was still crying, telling him how much he was missed and my regrets for not seeing him one last time. "But I am always still here," he told me. "I didn't really leave. I just went someplace else around here; it's not like

I'm really gone. Just always remember the stars," he added. "I do remember the stars," I said. "I love you and miss you, too," he said, "but don't be a sheep because you are like a lion. You have to live like you are supposed to live. Please stop this and go be happy in your life and don't worry about me." He continued to stroke my hair and then he kissed my lips. My body jerked and I suddenly woke up. The sun was shining on me through the blinds, my pillow was soaked with tears and my face was still wet. It all felt so real, the weight of his hands stroking my head, his lips on mine; I even smelled his cologne and heard his voice. Closing my eyes again, I tried to go back to sleep, hoping to get back to that place where I could see him again. But, of course, there was no going back to sleep. My mind was racing. Did that really happen or did I make it up? Is that even possible? Lying there for a moment, going over it in my head, I tried to remember all the details of what happened and how it felt. I was afraid to forget the details because things were already foggy and slipping away. I grabbed a notebook and started writing down the dream with as many details as possible, so that I wouldn't forget anything. I started to feel a bit happier and lighter and hopeful about things. My mind couldn't stop thinking about the experience. Was it possible for him to really visit me in the dream state?

I headed to the bookstore, looking for any books that could be found on life after death and encounters with people who had passed over. I discovered many other instances in which other people were claiming stories similar to mine happening after a loved one's death. Surprisingly, it was not uncommon at all. I found that some people believe dreams are the easiest way for spirits to visit and reassure loved ones.

A couple of days later, a deliveryman rang the doorbell and asked me to sign for a package. The package was from Majed. He must have sent it just prior to his accident. It was a beautiful necklace with small diamonds in a cluster that looked like a star. He used to say to me that no matter how far apart we were, it wasn't that far because we could always see the same stars. He loved looking at the stars, so the stars always remind me of him. Even today whenever I have the thought, I send love to them in case he's found a way to still share them with me.

My experience with this dream sparked my curiosity, and is responsible for my continuing interest and studies over the years about life after death. Eventually, my dream led me to Dolores Cannon's Past Life Regression work, which led me to believe that perhaps people don't really die, their souls just move on to something else, another place, or maybe a new life. To this day, I still fully believe, without a doubt, that my experience was real and a way for Majed to show me that everything was just fine. He, too, believed in prophetic dreams. He chose to come to me in a dream to show me that I needed to move on with my life and well, frankly, that I needed to get my butt out of bed and get on with it already.

Time marched on as it does and I went back to living my life like a lioness by taking on a number of new career challenges. Though still troubled, my heart was slowly continuing to heal. Little by little, I was pulling myself back together again emotionally. My focus was on the things and thoughts that made me happier and made me feel alive. As the dust began to settle, the expat life began calling to me again. I was ready for a new adventure. Traveling was still interesting, inspiring, and exciting for me. I recognized that as I became more aligned with the things that excited me and inspired my joy, the easier my life seemed and I was once again reminded that I could find happiness in my life.

My mind wandered with thoughts about going back to the Middle East. I began to put out feelers for jobs in Kuwait, maybe because being there made me feel closer to all the memories of Majed and, for some reason that country always felt like a peaceful home to me. I'm keenly aware of how strange that must sound with so many examples to the contrary, but for me, my external worldview is mostly driven by what is felt internally. I felt so much love and a great connection for the people, the culture, and the deserts. My choice was to focus on that love.

My bags were repacked and, before I knew it, I was back in Kuwait for a second time to live and work for a year or two. This time, I took a contracting job doing Cyber Security for the Army communications networks that supported the overall military efforts in the Middle East at Camp Arifjan. Going back to Kuwait helped me feel more at peace with myself over the loss of Majed, perhaps because I was closer to where he came from and where it all ended. I spent a lot of time in reflection about why we had never considered living in Kuwait together. It would have been much easier to accomplish logistically at that time. After all was said and done, there was a reason for my anxiety and fear leaving him that one last time in the airport, as well as for my hesitation to marry him and stay in Iraq longer. Deep down inside, despite the depth of the connection we felt for each other, we were never meant to be together forever. Intuitively, I think we both knew it all along, but don't we all want to believe that fairy tales come true? That we will meet someone that knocks us off our feet and against all the odds and life circumstances, that great love will prevail and we will live happily ever after and ride off into the sunset together? I do believe in the happy sunset ending, but knew it wasn't forever with him; it just took a while for me to admit that and kindly remind myself that tomorrow is never promised. We need to cherish the moments we have and be grateful for those in our lives, whether they were there for just a snap shot in time or longer. People come in and out of our lives, to love, serve, and learn, and when their role is done, sometimes they leave. Sometimes we have to leave. Saying good-bye to someone you know and have even loved hurts and is very difficult, regardless if they were in your life for several years, or just several months.

Kuwait felt like a second home to me, maybe because I had been through many life-expanding experiences there and had matured as a result. Being back, however, I found I was relearning and reassessing everything about myself. I gained even more recognition of the deep-seeded beliefs I held about what I valued and thought to be true. I found that even in my attempts to be open and willing to accept other cultures, I was still struggling with my judgment on some level about what I believed was right and wrong. My beliefs and behaviors regarding the culture were constantly challenged and, as always, there were plenty of opportunities to enjoy meeting and connecting with people from all over the world.

A little over a year had passed since my last stay in Kuwait and I noticed small changes taking place, the atmosphere even becoming more liberal. There were trees decorated for Christmas in the mall. Women were dressing a bit more fashionably and less modestly. Over the span of just a couple years, things were beginning to open up more. Even more malls were being built with new and recognizable franchises from the Western world cropping up, a difference from when I lived there previously.

Wanting to expand my daughter's horizons a bit, I convinced her father to allow her to spend a couple weeks with me in Kuwait. There was some resistance in the beginning. At that time, there was still a misguided and fearful theme of Westerners in the Middle East. And, of course, where my daughter was concerned—a beautiful, blonde-haired, blue-eyed 14 year-old—her father was within his bounds to worry about her safety. She had her doubts as well but trusted me and, in the end, had the courage to get on a nonstop flight by herself from Washington's Dulles Airport to Kuwait International Airport. Since my connections with Mohammad were still intact, he found a police officer friend to meet her at the gate as she was coming off the plane. He called me when he had found her and I let her know that she was safe to go with him and that he would take her through the immigration process and help her get the luggage.

He took her directly to the front of the visa purchase line and then she said he cut the line of people waiting to have their passports stamped. Being the airport police, no one questioned him or delayed them for one second. As the doors slid open I could see her walking down the walkway, luggage in tow, with the police officer beside her. It drew a bit of attention, but we ignored the gawking from the onlookers. I hugged her tightly, ecstatic to see her. Shaking the policeman's hand and thanking him, he nodded and then waved and walked off. I was so proud of her for having the courage to take that flight alone. It called for a large leap of faith.

During the time she was in Kuwait, we did some sightseeing. While driving to various sights, Jordan and her towhead blonde hair was a hit with the local population of teenage boys (and some grown men). We would be at a traffic light and the men in cars beside us would be locked in, gazing at her. When the light turned green, I would take off. Looking in the rear view mirror, we would laugh that they would still be sitting at the light after it had changed.

One evening as we were leaving the shopping mall on the marina, some teenage boys pulled their cars in front and behind us, effectively preventing us from leaving. They wanted to talk to Jordan. Irritated, I got out of the car and reminded them that what they were doing was against Allah, and they quickly retreated, getting out of the way and letting us pass by.

While walking down the street to visit the grocery store, we saw a man driving forward with his head completely turned to the side, staring at us as we walked. A few seconds later we heard a crash, and saw that he had run into the car in front of him, all due to his being distracted by my daughter and her obviously out-of-place blonde hair. All the attention put me on edge and on the defensive. Some grown men had no reservations about blatantly checking her out. Since she was only 14, I wasn't quite ready to see grown men eyeballing her in that manner.

Despite the constant attention from the locals, we had a great time together. Being able to show her another part of the world and way of life meant a lot to me. I believe it's important for children to travel and, if possible, be given these expansive experiences and viewpoints from other parts of the world. The exposure makes them wiser and kinder about their lives and other lives in this world. They are seeing real people, living real lives that don't look like theirs, and realizing they might have it pretty good after all. Or maybe they observe that the world isn't exactly what the people around them have told them. Either way, it's best for them to form their own opinions and experiences.

My good friend, Diana, came to Kuwait with me this time and ended up being my roommate in the housing provided by the company. She was also curious and interested in the cultural nuances of living as a woman in Kuwait. One day we had the idea of making a short documentary about the women of Kuwait. We wanted to show that they were just like other women, doing normal everyday things that Western women do, even though they might do things in a different way. We knew recording and taking pictures in public would be a challenge since there were laws against doing so. We decided to dress up like Kuwaiti women in full *abayas* with our faces covered. Taking the video camera with us to record each other doing normal things, we ventured out in the car. We noticed that with the *abaya* on and with our faces covered, we suddenly had a lot of younger Kuwaiti men trying to talk to us and get our attention while in traffic. They were trying to talk to us in Arabic and, of course, we had no idea what they were saying.

At one point we got the great idea to drive to a friend's apartment in another city and knock on his door to see his reaction. Driving down the highway, an older Kuwaiti man in a white sedan started tailgating us with his high beams on. He slid to the left side of our car and started motioning for us to pull over. I kept driving, reassuring Diana there was no way we were pulling over. It was late at night and we were on a part of the road where there was only desert and not much lighting. He pulled in front of us and put on his brakes and, as he did, I swerved over to the other lane passing him again. He came behind us and tried to hit us from behind. I started to get nervous because now it was serious; this guy was really attempting to run us off the road. He pulled to the left side of our car when I went to the right, and tried to push us off the road from the other side. There was no way we could outrun his car with our company vehicle and the faster we went the more dangerous the game became.

Suddenly, an idea came to mind and I told Diana, "I'm going to slow down and when he pulls to the right of us, take the video camera and point it at him and make sure he can see it." This time when he came around to the right, she brought up the video camera, and when she did he literally put his arm up to cover his face and swerved off the road, driving into the desert and away from us. We both started laughing hysterically. "What the heck was that!?" She exclaimed. I explained that Kuwaitis hated to be recorded or have their picture taken in public. "I'm glad it worked because he was determined to run us down," I said with a sign of relief.

Living and working in Kuwait was always a good jumping off point and a way for me to afford travel to see other countries and places around the world. I would be exhausted after coming home from a trip, with my money gone but well-spent. Not long after returning, I couldn't wait to find a new place to travel to. It was a never-ending curiosity inside of me that drove me to want to see the next thing. The expat lifestyle, even after ten years, never got tiring. At times, I still feel that yearning inside for an adventure abroad.

CHAPTER 10

European Living

"Each friend represents a world in us, a world possibly not born until they arrive, and it is only by this meeting that a new world is born."

— Anais Nin

After returning from my last Middle Eastern assignment, I spent time on United States soil for a few years. With fond memories of my experience in the Middle East, I was itching to live abroad once again. When the expatriate bug bites you, the itch is something that never really seems to go away. In between foreign assignments, I would circle back to the states for a year or two. Soon, I would get bored and begin looking for new places to live, experience, and explore. This lifestyle seemed to get easier as time went on and, as Jordan got older, she traveled with me. Improved technology also made it easier for us to communicate more regularly, no matter where I was in the world.

I had long dreamed about working in Europe. An opportunity for a position with NATO finally arrived two years after I originally applied. The assignment relocated me to The Hague, the Kingdom of the Netherlands. Within a few short weeks, my house was packed up with everything I owned easily fitting into a five-by-eight storage unit. With all my traveling and relocating throughout the years, I was accustomed to a more Spartan-like existence, reducing my living footprint and material possessions as much as possible. For me, furniture and other material things were a complication, weighing me down when the next big adventure came along. When it was time to move again (and I was always ready to move again), my packing and moving process was down to a science. My life could be neatly packed up in half of a day, so that by the next morning I could be on the move to a new life and career anywhere in the world.

This time around, there was a personal complication: a teary parting with my boyfriend, making it more difficult than usual to leave. A few years had gone by since Majed's death. Between focusing on my career and trying to spend time with my daughter, relationships seemed more complicated than ever. I desperately wanted to be in a meaningful relationship, but it was challenging to balance said relationship, while pushing forward in my career strives and dedicating time to my daughter. As a result, my personal life always seemed to be the lowest priority on the list. Even though we agreed to keep in touch and see each other every couple of months, I was left with a feeling that saying goodbye to him meant that, once again, I was choosing my career over a relationship. Yet, I couldn't see a way to balance both things without compromising the life I'd worked so hard to create. While I couldn't turn down this opportunity, I felt great sadness with this choice. There was also a lingering feeling of disappointment that I couldn't manage to have both, unlike others around me who seemed to hold it all together effortlessly. Why couldn't I have both? It seemed like I was always being forced to choose one or the other, happiness in my personal life or success in my professional life.

My life was a great adventure, far from the mundane. I was grateful for the life I had created for my daughter and myself. On my feet financially, we had great vacations, traveled internationally, and had done amazing things together. But even with all the success and opportunities, I was still lonely. There were more holidays spent without my family than I care to count. There was a longing for someone to share these great adventures with me.

For the time being, that all had to be put aside. Appearing calm and sure, I got on the plane ready to start a new adventure living in the Netherlands. Already knowing some people living in The Hague, it was easy for me to find a place to stay while looking for an apartment. There were plenty available, but I wanted one that would work for me. I found a three-bedroom apartment with large floor-to-ceiling windows that made it easy to take advantage of the elusive sun. I rented the second floor apartment from a nice Dutch family with three young boys who all looked alike. The parents were great landlords and quickly responded to any maintenance requests. Unlike many apartments in The Hague, mine had a washing machine, dryer, bathtub, a good-sized refrigerator, and a gas stove with a cooking range. Plus, the larger place suited me for when Jordan and my mother would join me in the summers.

After living in the apartment for a few months, I discovered that the Iranian embassy was three to four houses down the street. I immediately reported this fact to my intelligence officers at work. From that time on, I assumed that I was being watched. Weeks after my meeting with the intelligence officers, there was a group of expats that gathered to go bowling near the beach. I noticed that one dark-haired young woman with dark eyes was overly interested in me and tried hard to keep up the conversation between us throughout the night. She asked probing questions about my work, something that always put me on guard. I asked where she was from and she said, "Iran." Without looking surprised, I said, "Cool, why are you here? You're a long way from home." She told me that she worked on environmental issues with the oil industry. Since Shell's headquarters was also in The Hague, her explanation made sense. More red flags went up, however, when she followed me out of the bowling alley, insisting that we exchange contact information and keep in touch. She seemed to be working very hard to befriend me.

Heading home, my mind kept going over the conversation. The encounter bothered me so the next day at work I met with the intelligence officer again to report the encounter. Nothing more was heard from her after it was reported, and I never did see her again, but I became cautious of overly friendly people that were encountered and were curious about my work from that point forward. I wanted to believe that she was just trying to make friends. Unfortunately, given the tensions between the U.S. and Iran and where my employment was, her intentions had to be questioned. I didn't have the luxury to dismiss her as an eager friend, and didn't want to take any chances and get caught up in any international spy games. With all the embassies in The Hague, it's a breeding ground for spies and counter intelligence officers from every nation. It's safe to assume that every nation is collecting whatever information and intelligence they can get at all times.

At NATO, I was working as a cyber security engineer within a cyber security group. The role was about finding and addressing vulnerabilities and shortfalls in technology, providing support to command and control communications systems projects that were supporting various NATO missions. One of the biggest NATO-led security missions at the time was the International Security Assistance Force (ISAF) in Afghanistan. The UN Security Council established ISAF in 2001 to assist in the buildup and training of Afghan National Security Forces, and also to develop and mature some key government functions within Afghanistan. Beyond 2001, it became intertwined in the effort to deal with the Taliban insurgency by helping to secure Kabul and the surrounding areas from the Taliban, Al Qaeda, and other factions of warlords.

The Hague, located on the North Sea in the southern part of Holland, is an interesting place. Holland's third largest city, it has the most national embassies and more than 150 international organizations. The International Criminal Court is located there, and it is one of the four major locations for the United Nations. The first peace conferences took place in The Hague in the late 1800's, and they frequently tout themselves as the "international city of peace and justice," as well as the legal capitol of the world.

For the most part, the transition to that part of Europe was easy. Most of the Dutch speak English well enough. Holland is also widely known for its everyday use of bicycles for transportation. I quickly got on board and bought a bike to take advantage of the many well-established paths to and from work and shopping. I arrived in Holland at the end of April, the nicest time of the year, although the sunny days and good weather last only a few weeks. Because of The Hague's location on the North Sea, most of the year's weather is gray, damp, and cold, with the temperature averaging around 56 degrees Fahrenheit. After being caught in a torrential downpour one morning while riding to work, I purchased an inexpensive, used Alfa Romeo from a coworker. My Dutch colleagues would ask why I wasn't riding my bike to work as we watched the rain violently beat against our office windows. "It's raining sideways," I said. "You're kidding, right?" But they weren't kidding. Not only are the Dutch dedicated cyclists but it is a primary mode of transportation. They will ride their bikes in any weather, rain, snow, sleet or shine. As for me, not so much.

Actually, it took me some time getting used to riding a bike, or, for that matter, even walking downtown. The Hague was crowded, and there were so many activities on the streets, so much to watch out for people walking, cyclists, trolleys, buses, and cars. Rain or shine, the social scene in The Hague was pretty lively. With an embassy from every country and a large contingent of expats, there was always an event. There were weekly happy hours, gatherings, house parties, and weekend trips arranged to explore other parts of Europe. The railway is widely used in Europe, and is a convenient and inexpensive way to travel. Rather than use my car, I often took the train whether I was heading to the airport, taking a day trip to Amsterdam, Brussels, or another location that I wanted to visit throughout Europe.

Western Europe lived up to its reputation for being dark and rainy. My first summer there was one of the wettest and coldest, according to my Dutch friends and work colleagues. A serious case of homesick blues started to set in, exacerbated by communication troubles between me and my boyfriend. He started distancing himself and then just stopped writing or calling. He also didn't respond to my emails and calls. He quit the relationship cold turkey, with no explanation and no good byes. My American friends sympathized with me, calling it the relationship curse of The Hague. I was totally heartbroken at the time. When I left the U.S., we promised we would stay in close touch and see each other every few months, something that would take the sting out of a long distance relationship. He had apparently decided that this arrangement was not to his liking, but failed to discuss that with me before he disappeared. It made me question everything, even why I had chosen to go there for my career instead of staying back home and working on the relationship.

I had barely recovered from this breakup when I was forced to confront a number of health challenges that would ultimately see me fall into a deeper depression. The trouble began four weeks after arriving in The Hague when I severely sprained my ankle, rolling it while playing netball (a European version of basketball without dribbling). Making my way to the local International Health Centre (a small medical day clinic), I had my first experience with the Dutch medical system. I showed the doctor my ankle and she said, "Wow, that's bad! What would you like me to do?" This didn't seem like a good start. "What are my options?" I asked. "Shouldn't we x-ray this or something? I mean you're the doctor, you tell me!" She said, "Yes, ok, I'll write you a referral for an x-ray. On this doctor's order, I'll put two blocks here. If it's broken, check this block. If it's not broken, check here, and circle here for physical therapy." She was leaving me to fill in whatever I felt was needed on a doctor's order that she blindly signed. I went to the hospital for the x-ray.

Most of the signs in the hospital were in Dutch, and the officials at the entrance didn't speak English. I navigated my way hopping along on my good foot while dragging a painfully swollen ankle the size of softball. I finally located the right area of the hospital. The receptionist stared blankly at me as I asked for an x-ray and handed her my papers. The two ladies behind the counter spoke amongst themselves in Dutch for a couple of moments. One of them pointed at some chairs, and I took that as a signal to mean that I was expected to sit and wait, which I did. I waited for 45 minutes and watched as other people got called into the examination room. Everyone but me. My ankle was throbbing and sharp pains were shooting through my foot whenever I dared to move.

Finally it was my turn; they called my name and waved me into the room. The x-ray technician also spoke no English, so when we finished, she pointed back at the chairs. After sitting for another 45 minutes with my ankle throbbing in pain, the x-ray technician came out, looked at me and said, "Not broken." I had expected more information, but she went back into the room and slammed the door behind her. The receptionists stonewalled me.

By now, I was frustrated and angry. I walked down the hall trying to find someone, anyone who could help. My foot wasn't broken, but something was possibly torn or bruised since the swelling wasn't going down and the pain was unbearable. I knew something was needed—a splint, temporary cast, or soft boot, to protect and hold my foot in place.

I finally found someone who looked like a doctor and I explained my situation. At this point I felt that even tape would help me stabilize my ankle. "We don't have tape here," he told me before walking away. I shouted after him: "Oh sorry! I was under the impression I was in an actual hospital for a second."

With no other alternative, I hobbled across the parking lot to the pharmacy where athletic tape and ankle braces were being sold. As a basketball player in high school, I had watched athletic trainers tape a lot of ankles. I was able to mimic that process to provide some stability and relief for my ankle.

After a few weeks my ankle recovered, but my health problems were just beginning. The illnesses began with ear infections, a debilitating cold accompanied by a whooping cough, allergy symptoms that included headaches and a painful sinus infection. I experienced dizzy spells, stomach viruses, and flus that came with body aches and shivers for a week at a time. Even eating kabobs from street vendors in Baghdad had never made me this sick.

Needless to say, these illnesses did nothing to dispel the feelings of negativity and skepticism for what my life in The Hague had become. I began to question my reasons for being there. I had worked so hard to get to this point in my career. For what? Was this all that could be expected? Loneliness, sickness, and depression? It was a difficult pill for me to swallow. Why wasn't I feeling fulfilled or happy about how far I had come, and what had been achieved? My thinking took a dark turn, and I began to wonder why I was even on this earth. Not in a suicidal way, but in a searching and pissed-off-at-God kind of way. The conversation went something like this, "God, what is the point? Is this a race to live, work, pay taxes, have my heart broken, and endure sickness? Watch the people I love die? Then the ultimate grand finale is that I die? If so, I must tell you God, this kind of sucks! I blame you and think you kind of suck, too." I literally wrote, "God sucks!" I meant it at the time, too. I was not only asking what my purpose was for being there, but ultimately who I was and why all this struggle? If all of my previous ideals of happiness were proving to be untrue, then maybe I wasn't ever as happy as I thought. Or, perhaps I had outgrown my old definitions of happiness but I was too scared to exit the secure life of certainty I had worked so diligently to put together.

Whatever it was, life seemed like one big struggle and emotionally, I was a mess. Everything was up for questioning from my purpose, to other peoples' purpose, to who I was and how I fit into this world, and what was the point of it all? Previously, I identified myself as this hardworking, career-minded woman who was strong and tireless, and could take on anything in life and win, including winning my dream job. That career now felt more like a golden cage. It didn't matter how far up that ladder I climbed, it was a sobering reality that my happiness couldn't be found where I had been looking for it, and because of that life felt useless.

As time went on, I became increasingly depressed, angry, lonely, and pretty darn pitiful. My good friend David, who would take me on short trips to new cities and shopping, tried to cheer me up with new places to visit. Those outings would temporarily distract me from my internal pain, but my heart still felt broken on multiple levels. My thoughts kept rerouting back to the same place: All of these things in my life and I'm not any happier than I was living in public housing 15 years ago. What is wrong with me? This loop of thinking aggravated my situation, creating even more stress. There were days when the anxiety was so high, it felt like I was having a heart attack, with sharp chest pains deep in my heart.

I had no idea what to do or what was happening to me; and, on top of it all, the guilt started to set in that I was a grown woman who didn't know how to make herself happy. How could I feel so unappreciative and even resentful of my life? Shouldn't my life be happy? Living this life in Europe was what I had dreamed about and wanted. If that didn't do it, would anything ever make me happy?

It seemed like everything I went after and wanted in life came to me. Every next thing pursued always arrived. When pausing to question why it meant so much to me to have it, I realized that there was a belief that happiness looked a certain way. That certain way always looked like what I didn't seem to have yet. It always looked like the next thing I was trying to get, but when I got it, it felt empty. The next career move, bump up in salary, relationship, outfit or even the next new car. Once I got it, it still didn't give me any more peace or happiness. As a result of this feeling, I thought that maybe happiness was always just outside of my grasp, and life started to feel like a cruel joke. I felt alone, exhausted and couldn't find the sweetness of life anywhere. Everywhere I looked, whether with my personal friendships, my tasks at work, or the community I lived in, more reasons to be unhappy and depressed kept showing up.

Of course, I wasn't ready to throw in the towel, and there were attempts made to get out of the sadness rut I was in. One night, after receiving an invitation to a birthday party, I decided to get dressed up and go out on the town with some friends. The combination of really high heels and one too many martinis resulted in my taking a good fall down some treacherous Dutch stairs. It was a pretty nasty tumble that left me in quite a lot of pain in my lower back, pelvis, and shoulder. Later I discovered there were serious injuries as a result of the fall: I had two herniated discs, my pelvis was twisted, and my shoulder had started to become frozen from landing on my elbow. I could not get the doctor at the clinic in The Hague to write me a referral for an MRI to find out the extent of the injuries, so I lived with the pain for several months. I saw a number of medical professionals, including natural doctors, physical therapists, and chiropractors, but none helped me very much. They tried acupuncture, needling, adjustments, and homeopathic methods. Nothing helped the pain, which made it impossible for me to sleep more than a few hours at a time. I had been suffering with pain and discomfort for more than six months. Not being able to sleep meant that my mood became even darker and impatience grew with those around me. If you have ever been in chronic pain, you understand that it goes beyond dealing with the physical pain. There's a psychological effect as well. I was exhausted and began to feel desperate about my situation. Life seemed beyond bleak.

David insisted on getting me help. He put me in his car and drove me to the American Hospital in Paris. Within four hours, they ran many tests and finally had a diagnosis. The chief of surgery proposed to remedy the lower back with a cortisone shot in my spine, which then caused the worst sciatica pain I have ever experienced in my life, from the top of my hip to the tip of my toes. Following the shot, the sciatica got worse and added to the constant pain. Surgery was suggested, but the doctor said the procedure might not work. He then delivered the final blow: that I could be in pain the rest of my life, regardless of his efforts.

Despite the doctor's misguided attempts to help me, I have to thank him for one suggestion: the recommendation to investigate alternative healing methods, saying that many people found relief with such treatments when traditional Western medicine wasn't working for them. He said that he had seen people continue to live active lives using alternative healing methods as "pain management." Vehemently opposed to surgery, I slowly began to realize that whatever was going on with me might be fixed naturally. I just needed to figure out what form that "fix" would take.

I ended up being stuck in Paris on bed rest for another three or four weeks. David, who was from Paris, found me a lovely efficiency apartment in an affordable and decent part of the city. As I spent time there attempting to recover, lying flat while staring at the ceiling, I made promises to myself that when my health was back, I was going to live a different life. Being happy was going to be my top priority, and I would do whatever necessary to make those changes to my life. Whatever direction my life took, it meant doing something more meaningful, impactful, and helpful to others. The arrival of this conclusion was met by the idea that if I felt this way about my life, then others might also feel this desperation and pain in some way as well. Maybe once I helped myself, I could find a way to share that help with others.

Just having a diagnosis made me feel more positive and in a better place mentally. At least now I knew what was wrong with me physically. My thoughts quickly went to the energy work I had encountered in the past at the Open Door. I remembered people's bones moving back into place and remembered the possibility that the body could heal itself. There were many stories of people with injuries much worse than mine, accidents that even left some people completely paralyzed. Yet, after being told they would be wheelchair-bound for life, some of these people were able to walk again. These cures were described as miracles. But I was convinced that these spontaneous healings, or "self-healings," as some say, aren't really miracles at all. The body is going to do what it was designed to do, which is to heal. It's what the body can do when it is out of balance or out of harmony. Sometimes the body is spinning too many plates in the air at once, essentially multitasking. The multitasking can begin to compromise the body's natural ability to regain its balance. In addition, if the heart and mind aren't working in concert with the body, it takes longer, if ever, to reverse the imbalance. Most people don't know how to access or inspire their own healing potential by themselves, and this is where a catalyst is needed to remind them.

Finally returning back to The Hague, I began researching intently. As the doctor suggested, I began trying various alternative-healing methods, hopeful I'd find a remedy that might help encourage the healing process for me. I continued to see homeopaths, chiropractors, physical therapists, and acupuncturists, but didn't see much improvement. I was still unable to stand straight or sit for too long without pain. Emotional turmoil reigned within me, which continued to make it difficult to sleep well. My boss was less than impressed with my time away from the office. Now I had to also deal with the rolling eyes from colleagues, and the raised eyebrow from the little self-appointed Napoléon personality at work. My otherwise sharp mind was not at all feeling sharp; it was cloudy. I was incredibly short-fused, irritable, and quick to anger. Constantly attempting to manage the feeling of exhaustion, above any other activity in my life, I couldn't wait to crawl into bed.

After finishing with all the physical manipulations, acupuncture, therapeutic machines, and cortisone shots, there was still something drawing me to the more ethereal and natural ways of healing. My intuitive feeling was that whatever I needed to find was more profound than anything yet to be experienced. My searches online about energy healing yielded some interesting results. Having already experienced some success with energy healing in the past, I felt that if the healer was good enough, whatever their methods, then I could be helped.

My research led me to discover a few energy healers locally and I visited each for one-on-one treatment. They all took their best shot at my laundry list of complaints. I would experience a day or so of improvement with one of the healers, but nothing really stuck. After a day or so, the pain would return. A few things actually freaked me out. One spiritual healer said healing was impossible for me because of bad karma in my family. He wasn't allowed to go further into details about that because "they," the people he was connecting with in the spiritual realms for information, weren't letting him see any more. Another lady told me my chakras were broken, so she did a chakra "adjustment" to put them back together again, but indicated it was a really tough job, which would require several more visits. I didn't notice improvement after leaving her office: my pain level was the same and I experienced no improvements to my emotional state or sleeping habits. I did have to immediately change my clothes as they reeked of cigarette smoke, because she chain-smoked in her waiting room where she greeted her patients. There was another lady who did long-distance healing work. She insisted that her patients be sleeping while she worked on them. So we agreed on a night and I slept as best I could. But after waking up, no changes were noticed from her treatment either.

After trying nearly every type of energy healing master in the region, I was frustrated and nearly ready to give up. Then I stumbled upon a video. There was a website linked to it with more information about the benefits of a healing modality called PureBioenergy Therapy. The ideas expressed and shown in the video aligned with what I had been sensing and feeling about how the body would be able to heal itself. Without ever hearing of this modality before, I made a split-second decision to enroll in the class, which took place near London's Hyde Park just a week or so away. Additionally, I scheduled a healing session with the master and teacher of the class, Zoran Hochstatter, while attending his training.

Unlike other methods I'd come across over the years, there was something intriguing and different about this energy healing technique. The videos and testimonies seemed impressive and, more importantly, the approach seemed to align with the kind of results I was expecting from an energy healing experience. I kept thinking yes! Energy healing IS this powerful! The question was, would it work for me, and would I be able to do it?

Showing up for the first day of class and healing session with Zoran, I was jittery. What if the process didn't work on me? What if I was too resistant, stubborn, or not open enough? What if my problems were too complicated? I hoped he could help me. A man with a white beard and long, white, shoulder-length hair walked into the room. He was indeed the man from the video. He looked like a healer, but was wearing normal clothes — a T-shirt, and blue jeans. There wasn't an overt mysticism about him. Barely acknowledging me or the other three people present, he moved deliberately around the room, setting up a laptop and chairs. He finished preparing for the session, looked up and asked, "Who is having therapy today?" Seeing me raise my hand, he motioned for me to come to where three chairs were lined up perfectly side-by-side and in a row. The precision of the set-up and formality of how he behaved reminded me a bit of the military. He introduced himself, and chatted with me for a few minutes. I noted to myself that he seemed like a normal, down-to-earth guy who had no sign of being untethered from the earth, as I had experienced with other healers in the past. Other than the eccentric hair, he didn't seem to fit the mold of any other healer I had experienced. I continued to study him while he asked the reason for my visit. I rattled off my long list of ailments: back pain from two herniated discs in the lower back; pelvis pain from the fall; constant sciatica pain shooting from hip to toe; frozen shoulder; elbow pain; exhaustion; fatigue from sleep deprivation; debilitating painful menstrual cycle; depression; ankle pain (still); emotional distress; and an overall general displeasure with my life. He looked at me with no expression or concern and said, "Is that it?" Surprised by his lack of concern for my problems, I said, "Well, I guess that is it." Maybe it was too much for him to contend with? I added, "If you just can fix the sleep thing, I would be eternally grateful, and consider that alone a big success." Barely acknowledging the request, with an "uh-huh," he nonchalantly chewed a piece of gum, walked to his laptop and turned on some classic rock music. Then he went to work and began the healing session.

Standing in front of me, he waved his arms around me and I began to sway and rock back and forth. I quickly stopped myself. Should I be moving? Was it normal, real, or my imagination? Unfazed by my movement, he continued. If he wasn't concerned, I guess there was no need for me to be—after all, it was clear he knew what he was doing and was in charge of the situation. He continued to move around me, making hand movements I'd never seen before.

179

I was feeling wobbly but decided not to tell him. He placed his hand on my forehead and now something was definitely happening. Once again, my body started swaying back and forth. The movement was involuntary, out of my control. I wasn't making my body move and he wasn't physically pushing me. His hands were barely resting on my head. Within a couple seconds, the movement began again, and the swaying became more intense. Simultaneously, an intense wave of relaxation was coming over me and for the first time in as long as I could remember, a deep sense of calm internal peace settled inside of me.

He sat me down for the next phase of the treatment and made more hand movements in front of my heart and across my whole body. There was a sensation of blissfulness and an almost eerie stillness settling inside of me, right where all the busy internal chatter had lived. Before I knew it, the session was over. Disappointment swept over me. "Oh dear, it's over?" I said to myself. "This feeling is amazing and I don't want it to end." I was riding the blissful wave of euphoria, unable to understand what exactly had transpired. Without being able to explain what had happened, I was content.

He didn't speak to me during the treatment. There was no machine and nothing was ingested. It was a guy, doing this seemingly deliberate hand waving around me. It was odd and different, and, at the same time, looked elegant and effortlessly simple. The feeling of peace and calmness inside of me was something that had seemed elusive for a long time, and I loved it.

After we were finished with the therapy session, the class got underway and Zoran began with student introductions and then a lecture. The things he said in his lecture about health, wellness, and life struck a chord of truth deep within me. This was confirmation. I felt it in every fiber of my being. Feelings are sometimes difficult to express or put into words, especially when searching for an explanation to match what you feel. Often, the things I saw externally were incongruent with what I felt to be right or true internally. But what he said in his lecture made simple sense and was in total alignment with what I had been feeling or knowing as true. He spoke about focus, and how thoughts are energy. By focusing thoughts on a problem, we make problems bigger. Equally, by focusing on solutions, we will find plenty of larger solutions. He talked about positive and negative aspects of energy, and how energy is just energy. Positive and negative are just a measure, as in too much of something or too little. However, energy itself is neutral, it just is.

I began to grasp the concept that, in order to heal there is no need to describe or categorize illness as good or bad, containing clean or dirty energy. The judgment of characterizing someone's energy as dirty or clean expands that specific label in either direction, not only diminishing the healing results, but also impacting the healer, leaving that person exhausted, fatigued, and susceptible to illness. Oftentimes, healers tuning in that way can become drained of their health and need healing themselves to regain their balance. Healers are not superhuman or immune to illness, that's why it is important to learn how to heal others without being pulled into alignment of the frequency of the illness. The need to "cleanse" oneself can be eliminated when staying congruent with life force energy that is all around us. There's nothing purer than life itself. If you hold yourself in the light, nothing else you are holding can be in darkness. Good and bad, light and dark exist; in fact, one can't exist without the context of another. But as Zoran says, "It's just different sides of the same coin." What's important, not only as a healer but also in life, is which side of the coin you are placing your focus and intention.

The premise of the method is based on the therapist's ability, through a few basic steps and specific hand movements, to channel in new information, or source energy, to the client. The part that I feel takes the most practice is promptly stepping aside so the healing can happen. As healers, we act only as the delivery mechanism of the information, i.e.: source energy, prana, chi, and ki. In other words, it is coming to the understanding that we are not the ones doing the healing; we are simply holding the space, or frequency, for the client's body to heal. The frequency and information contained in the energy inspires the body back to the true and naturally intended way of being, which is wellness. Ultimately, the healer is merely the messenger, and actively exercising humility of that fact by staying out of nature's way.

If you cut yourself, you may bleed and when the bleeding stops, your skin begins to generate new skin over the open wound. Soon you will have a scab, and then slowly that disappears and maybe you will have a scar, and then the scar fades. I'm pretty sure no one has ever called this a miracle; this is the natural healing process of the body; nature's way. I think it's generally understood that the body will heal itself naturally, until we start talking about bigger things that conjure up fear (like cancer), and suddenly some of society believes that healing is much more of an undertaking, requiring reliance on something much more complex. Perhaps it is in some cases, however I still propose that even in the most difficult cases, the healing process can be much simpler than we have been led to believe.

There are many other forms of healing modalities around the world; they all serve a purpose and on some level, they all work, especially if they lead people to remember themselves for who they are in a true and authentic way. Whatever approach is used, maybe it's chosen based on various desired outcomes or results. Some results are better than others. As our knowledge and understanding evolve, so do new possibilities.

People do what they know, and maybe sometimes a better way isn't known yet. We all have our own truth, and our own ways of approaching wellness on our journey. The experience that I'm living out has to do with becoming really honest about the truth of who I am, my divine nature (as opposed to my egoic self), taking responsibility for my own health and happiness, and showing up in the most authentic way possible so others may also feel safe to do the same.

The most important point of all of this is that, from a practical perspective, bodies heal themselves. Perhaps the Dutch medical process is on to something after all, but maybe they are missing the piece where they educate people how to achieve their desired level of health and wellness *after* the injury has occurred.

After all this time searching, it felt like I had finally found my Tribe, a place to fit in with a group of people that knew there was more potential to natural healing and wellness than what the mainstream medical establishment had conceded. Now, there were endless possibilities and outcomes. This knowledge to help others heal literally made me cry. I cried because I was happy to have found it, and because of how deeply the simplicity of it resonated once I heard it.

After the second day of therapy, I woke up the following morning, looked at the clock and realized that I had slept a full eight hours without waking up! Getting out of bed, I noticed there was no pain in my back or hip. There was still tightness and a bit of pain in my shoulder as I dressed. After finishing breakfast and suddenly feeling tired, I went back to my room to rest before class started. Lying on the bed, everything I had learned in class the day before came into my mind. Still enamored by the simplicity of the method, I suddenly began laughing out loud. "Of course healing is this simple!" Then came more uncontrollable, hysterical laughing out loud, and I have to admit that I was even howling with laughter — on my own — in my hotel room. After 15 minutes of laughing, I began sobbing. I turned the television on to mask the sound, afraid my laughing and crying would wake the guests in other rooms. Then the laughing started again; then the sobbing. This laughing and crying spell went on for about an hour. My abdominal muscles were aching, my head was spinning, and I thought I was losing it. When it finally all stopped and my emotions settled, there was a pile of used tissues crumpled up all over the bed, along with a huge sense of relief. It was as if the weight of the world had been lifted from my shoulders.

Standing up, I rolled my shoulders front to back and lifted my arm. The full range of motion was back in my shoulder. Drying my face and blowing my nose one more time, I acknowledged that the pain was completely gone from my back. My heart and mind felt synchronized, and I felt a profound impression of peace, overwhelming joy, and gratitude. The excitement at the possibility of being able to help others, as I had been helped, gave me a renewed sense of the possibilities in my life.

After the remaining time in class and the remainder of the sessions, my pain level dropped from a constant nine in the beginning (ten being the worst) to a one or barely even there. After another day or so, the pain was completely gone. Upon returning to Holland, it was hard to conceal my excitement about how good I was feeling. For the first time in almost a year I was walking upright, without a limp. People in my office noticed the difference and asked what had helped me. I started telling people about my healing, eager to share the therapy with friends. Soon, people were showing up at my house at night wanting to experience the healing work. They had heard and seen the rapid healing results that had happened to me and were curious to experience it for themselves. It started with two or three people, and soon there were 10 to 15 people showing up. I became so busy that a weekly schedule was set up. The first 40 people or so that tried the energy healing with me were my trial cases. Could I do it? Was I doing it right? The people who came believed in this treatment after seeing what had happened to me. But were they really healing, or just being polite by saying their pain was gone? There were a lot of questions coming up as I was doing this work.

Yet, I was unable to argue with the results. People not only healed, they started telling others. I made plenty of mistakes in the beginning. After all, I was just learning the basics at that stage, and my curiosity kept me moving forward. Even so, we were seeing amazing healing results with each and every case that was brought to me.

I offered sessions to my landlord's wife and kids who lived below me. Their mom told me they had trouble sleeping at night and difficulty focusing in school. One of the children who had anxiety was less social and refused to get a haircut. He was constantly wearing a hooded sweatshirt with his bangs covering his eyes. On the first day of the therapy, all three boys enjoyed the treatment and felt the energy. They were swaying and moving. On the second day, their mom reported better sleep, lighter moods, and more laughter all around. By the third day, the hooded sweatshirt was off, and the boy asked for a haircut. By the fourth day, they were no longer using sleep medications, and the teacher called the mom to ask what she had done. Apparently there were some serious behavioral challenges with one of her sons, resulting in the mom having to go to the school a couple of times a week to meet with the teacher. The teacher noticed right away that something was different, and told the mother to keep doing whatever she was doing because it worked.

I had spent a lot of time asking myself the purpose of my life. Why am I here? The reason began unfolding right before my eyes. Being healed and learning to help others heal gave me my life back, putting me back together again so to speak. Everything in my external life stopped feeling like a struggle, maybe because everything inside of me stopped feeling like a struggle. I didn't feel the need to fight my way through life anymore. The idea of consciously living with purpose helped me regain balance in my life. I started a journey helping others find their wholesome balance in life and return to a few basic, but very important, concepts in life, concepts that might even have been previously discounted because of their simplicity.

CHAPTER 11

It's All Energy

"Everything is energy, your thoughts begin it, your emotion amplifies it and your action increases its momentum."

— Unknown

Life is simple, but isn't often easy. Sometimes it takes a while to discover that we are (unintentionally) preventing ourselves from healing. The thoughts and beliefs I held on to so tightly are what stifled my natural healing process. Long after I realized that my outlook and beliefs had compounded my illness, it still took me time to really understand the connection and the conflicts those beliefs and that outlook caused, much less change them. As a result, I was hard on myself, often overly-judgmental and critical of my inability to just get better. It took a long time to step away from this self-blame and judgmental behavior.

In doing healing work for others, my self-judgment and blame began to deconstruct. I was easier on myself, and therefore learned not to judge people based on their struggles with the human condition. Most people don't know how to move beyond an illness alone and are just doing the best they can to deal with it all. What they need more than judgment regarding what's going wrong in their life is compassion, understanding, and gentle reminders of their great potential. In fact, for best results, I focus upon each person's perfect and well human spirit because that is the truth of who we really are. Illness is just an assertion that has been made (either subconsciously or consciously) outside of the principle fact of their well-enduring human spirit.

The healer's thoughts are an important part of the equation. A healer who begins by judging is now in cahoots with the untrue assertion that the client has made about himself or herself, which perpetuates the existence of the imbalance. As soon as the healer deems the situation negatively, or attempts to rank its severity, the healer has unintentionally reinforced the energy of the issue at hand. In order to judge it, you would have to be in alignment to it. Even displeasure of the issue is alignment that is creating reinforcement in the form of resistance or opposition. We can't claim to love each other and ourselves, and then judge someone's out-of-balance condition or illness as bad. Perhaps the illness or the imbalance was necessary to their evolution? We can't possibly begin to know what someone's journey is all about; that is their truth to discover. The job of the healing is not necessarily to remove the illness, but to remind and realign the person's true self. The side effect of the realignment is the disappearance of the illness. In this way we are not actually addressing illness, but the wellness in each person we touch.

While walking down the healer's path and receiving my own layers of healing as a result, I started becoming more aware of the diversity of people's perspectives, ideas, and even objections about how wellness and healing occur.

One thing I've found to be interesting is when people say they don't believe in all these "energy things," especially energy healing. I've heard it from both religious and nonreligious people and even from pragmatic and logical people. I've heard it from those in the scientific community and from people who, in many other ways, would be considered open to nonconventional ways of thinking. Naysayers come from all socio-economic backgrounds and from all ethnic groups. When a religious person tells me that only God can heal, I like to respond: "How do you know that God didn't arrange our meeting?" Some need to understand how it all works before they can trust or believe. Some people aren't ready to hear it yet, and some will never be ready. Perhaps what I'm doing (or what other healers are doing) will never resonate for them; maybe it's not part of their journey. The biggest part of my growth happened when I genuinely stopped caring about who questioned and opposed it, and just began focusing on those who asked for my help and were willing to receive my help when it was offered.

Much to my dismay, even my closest and dearest longtime friends didn't believe that I helped several people reverse the effects of PTSD. I've had the opportunity to work with both veterans and civilians suffering with the effects of the diagnosis of Post-Traumatic Stress Disorder (PTSD), and the clients have had significant successes in returning to wellness. PTSD is an arduous diagnosis to live with, not only for those who suffer with it, but also for those living with sufferers. The psychological and emotional effects are debilitating and have left thousands of military veterans in despair and desperate for relief. Post-traumatic stress is not limited to those in the armed forces; civilians can suffer from it as well. It can affect anyone who has experienced a traumatic event; witnessing trauma of any kind can cause the long-lasting effects of PTSD.

While scrolling down my newsfeed on Facebook, I read an old schoolmate's post about a severe burn she received in an electrical fire caused by the dryer in her home. As she was struggling to quickly put out the flames, her hand was fiercely singed. I sent her a private message offering her a session with me to see if it could aid in the healing process, possibly prevent her scheduled surgery. I've found that it's a shot in the dark offering this help to people and not knowing if they will accept it or gaff me off like I'm some kind of a snake oil salesman. In this case, my friend eagerly agreed to the treatments. She also revealed that she suffered from PTSD following her father's unexpected and tragic suicide. After his death, she experienced great emotional trauma after having to clean up the remnants of blood in her father's home. Just five years prior, she had also experienced the suicide of a very close and dear friend of hers. She had the fury of one emotional turmoil after another, all the while trying to keep her life together for the two children she was raising as a single mother.

After starting the treatments, she noticed a significant change in how she felt and how her wounded hand looked right after the first session. Upon completing the four days of therapy, she had a wonderful healing result, and wrote a gracious testimony of her experiences:

For weeks, I have been trying to come up with the right words to describe my experience with working with Darcy. To say it changed my life would be an understatement, and how could I possibly explain it to someone who has never experienced it? Life changing is the first word that comes to mind. I do have to admit; I didn't really know what I was in for when I agreed to do the healing sessions, and it was far more intense than I had dreamed possible. Not only did it heal my physical ailments, but it healed my psyche as well.

Her story is not uncommon, others with PTSD that received this therapy also felt transformed. The symptoms that had once controlled their lives abated, allowing them to sleep better, stay calm, and feel "normal" again. Maddeningly, when I described and shared the great healing results with friends, the response was, "I doubt you could actually do that." Since these are people who consider themselves spiritually enlightened and open, I perceived their lack of faith was a lack of faith in me and not in the possibility of PTSD being reversed. On some level, I could understand their doubts. I'm not special or a Chosen One doing the healing. I'm a regular person who has learned and cultivated a skill. The process of helping another heal isn't about being special, instead—for me—it's about being dedicated to learning a process until success outweighs defeat. Few people are born knowing how to pragmatically tap into life-changing healing modalities. There are well-known healers who were born with realization of their exceptional healing abilities, but they are few and far between. The rest of us must learn these skills over time through practice and dedication.

Maybe some people are on a path that requires them to believe that a chronic illness should always involve a long, drawn-out struggle, that healing can't possibly happen with something as simple as energy. That is their journey, and I honor them in that journey as well. I understand that when people suffer, they may feel helpless and, as a result, breaking that cycle of pain and illness seems impossible. I lived with both external and internal pain for years. It ain't no picnic, but it doesn't have to be permanent.

Energy healing is easily overlooked as an effective form of therapy because it seems so subtle. After all, medical doctors spend a small fortune studying for decades towards a degree. They commit their lives to becoming experts in understanding illnesses; therefore, it should be as equally complicated and costly to deliver all forms of healing, right? In that framework it sure seems to be. Others, one day, realize that possibilities outside of known frameworks can work just as well, or even better, to eliminate or reduce struggles with most illnesses.

People have to decide what works for them and whether they can or want to open their hearts and minds to try something outside of the Western mainstream philosophy. If someone isn't open to another way, it isn't wrong. It is never wrong to pursue what you believe to be right for you, whatever you choose that to be. That is your freedom of choice, and I respect that everyone lives from a place of choice.

At the start, understanding other people's right to choice was difficult. When I began helping people, my ideas were at times met with condescension, especially when trying to describe what I was doing. I understood then that it was not my job to convince anyone of anything. I'm more like a spokesperson for an alternative approach to life, and whoever resonates with that truth listens.

Perhaps this is the result of years of conditioning and framing and it isn't easily undone. These ideas I'm presenting about healing and life in general can challenge people's deeply held beliefs and reality, and that can be very uncomfortable to sit with. My reaction was the same way when I first sought help for my medical situation. I was fearful of the consequences of my injuries and in a lot of pain. I first turned to what was familiar before seeking out alternative methods. My hesitancy prolonged my healing process and almost thrust me into the medical loop-de-loop of pills and surgery.

Solutions can come to us in many different forms if we are in a space of allowing. Making presuppositions to the Universe that things can only happen a certain way creates a constraint that diminishes the availability of possible outcomes.

According to Einstein's formula, (E: energy, M: mass, C: speed of light, squared) mass and energy are one and are interchangeable. In other words, everything with mass is energy; everything with energy can be mass. If we accept that theory, then, essentially everything we do, create, believe, think, and say is, in fact, energy. People may not perceive it that way because, most of the time, we are experiencing the end result (our outward picture) of the full manifestation of that energy in a solid state: energy materialized into solid matter. Everything leading up to the creation of a physical thing — whether it is the thought, concept, process, or framework — began as energy, an intangible fragment existing only in the mind. The density of the object is a matter of vibration and frequency. At a certain frequency range of the matter, we begin to see an object.

Another way to think about frequency ranges is with sounds. Many sounds can be naturally detected with the human ear, yet there are many frequencies of sound that are outside of the range of what can be heard. As indicated with dog whistles—which are indistinguishable to the human ear—dogs are able to hear at much higher frequencies than humans. Would it be unreasonable to assert that there might be other frequencies within the spectrum that the four human senses are unable to perceive? On some level, couldn't they exist?

Energy also can be used to promote the natural healing of the human body. The body, made up of billions of cells (mass), is also energy. Each cell is made up of molecules, and those molecules are made up of atoms vibrating back and forth at a certain frequency. The frequency is what creates the overall resonance of that cell. Groups of cells make tissues, which make organs, bones, blood, and the other stuff that forms the body, all vibrating and resonating as one unified frequency. The body itself is vibrating at the frequency of health or it is vibrating at the frequency of illness, or some variation within that spectrum.

When we say we are doing "energy healing," what that means to me is that we are raising our frequencies to a frequency of wellness. At a high enough frequency, lower level frequencies can't continue to exist and start to rise to match the higher frequency.

Looking at traditional medicine, does the average person understand what chemical process occurs in the body when a pill is ingested? Most people swallow pill after pill on their doctor's orders without understanding what's happening inside their body or how taking that pill will lead to healing. The pill, too, is matter or energy in physical form. The pill, however, doesn't find the root of the problem and resolve it. The pill is the delivery mechanism of information, attempting to provoke the body's immune system into doing what it is designed to do— heal itself. The pill itself doesn't directly heal; it instigates the immune system to get to work on the issue. There are side effects with pills, as adequately pointed out at the end of every TV commercial or in the fine print under each magazine advertisement, and rightly so, since certain things aren't natural or organic to the human body.

Regardless of what method is used, or how the body is inspired and moved from a state of illness to a state of wellness, it's important to note that it's all energy. Sometimes, when the body doesn't recover, heal, or change states from illness to wellness, it's because the body needs more information. Maybe the immune system is so badly taxed that it cannot overcome the issues it is facing quickly enough, compromising its full potential of healing functionality. This can be due to any number of things, like the environment or repetitive habits that do not support wellness of the body. In my case, there certainly needed to be a catalyst and an effective delivery mechanism for the information to inspire the body to get to work and heal itself, and I'm beyond grateful that I found something to get me there.

The pill, the procedure, or the energy healing process; no matter what you choose for yourself when it comes to healing is just fine, but there is only one process that occurs in every single human being, going from the state of illness to the state of wellness, and that is *your body is doing the healing.*

CHAPTER 12

Where Healing Happens

"Tell me and I'll forget, show me and I may not remember, involve me and I'll understand."
—Ruxio, Teachings of the Ru
By: Liu Xiang quoting Xun Kuang teachings

Working as a healer is transformational. Not just from a physical standpoint but also mentally, and especially emotionally. When I was able to help others heal, it started to transform my life. It's rewarding helping others to remember the truth of who they are by helping them find their inner balance of wellness, peace, and joy. The far-reaching effects of doing healing work conditioned me to recognize the positive side of living. With the internal confusion and chatter silenced, awareness of who I truly am was a deep recognition that supported me in making personal changes necessary to step into acceptance of who I am today.

Feeling better and calmer day-by-day, I didn't sweat the small stuff anymore, and, as they say, everything was small stuff. I smiled more, played more, and made a completely new circle of friends. It didn't happen harshly or abruptly, it's just that the old friends didn't work; either they called me crazy and didn't understand what I was doing, or froze me out by discontinuing contact. Others just faded away as life took its natural turns and progressions. One day I noticed they weren't there, and it was perfectly okay. When you begin doing this type of work, the Universe has a funny way of putting your life into alignment; the integrity of this work commands as such. If I was unable to say goodbye to a person or a situation that was no longer healthy for me, the Universe obliged by doing the dirty work and it quickly dissipated, happening seemingly without effort on my part.

I started behaving and taking care of myself differently, making different food choices, resolving emotional conflicts and any other unhealthy situations in my life. There was a new level of respect for myself that I hadn't recognized before. The old ideas I once held about what my life had to look like and who I had to be were gone. These individual changes may seem trivial, but, together, resulted in a peaceful way of being in my life and interacting with others.

As I continued to work with clients and observe the healing, there was a growing appreciation and gratitude for how wonderful my life truly was. Coming to surface were emotional memories I had internalized as a young child, which I had been holding onto and even forgetting about for over two decades. Viewing these memories from a fresh vantage point, without being forced to relive any pain no matter how bad the memory, I found a different, happier perspective. When a memory surfaced, I would often chuckle at my childhood innocence, forgiving myself with a bit of compassion for how it was naively held. The memory would then be gone, softly fading away, as if I was letting go of the string of a helium balloon and watching it soar into the blue sky.

The more work I did on others, the more I came to a grander place of self-acceptance. Initially, my intent was to help others heal but I eventually understood that each person I helped was also helping me. By allowing me to co-create wellness and health within others, the process took me outside of myself. It got me out of my own head by focusing on being of service to someone in need.

With each person I found myself fascinated by the results. I celebrated the healing results with my clients, feeling completely elated while watching their speedy return to wellness. Within the first year, I performed hundreds of treatments. Little did I know just how much impact observing all of these seemingly miraculous recoveries would have on my personal health. By working with others, I was actually introducing myself to the frequency of wellness and constant possibilities of healing over and over again. The result of my healing could have never been touched to this level, much less resolved by traditional methods or talk therapies in this lifetime. Having tried many of the traditional methods myself over the years, this alternative method seemed to fast track my results without the uncomfortable digging, discussing, and re-experiencing.

My personal results were a better sense of my being, of who I truly was on the inside, and a keener understanding of my priorities and gratitude for everything, even for the difficult path that got me there.

I spent a few more months in Europe doing healing work in my living room after work. I was still in shock that this could actually be done with my two hands, and that it was so effortless and simple. It felt like an amazing gift had been given to me and I couldn't wait to share it with the world.

With a few good successes and the excitement of this newfound healing ability, my mind was racing at all the possibilities that lay ahead. My thoughts went quickly to the military, my former community, which was struggling with Post-Traumatic Stress Disorder (PTSD) and other conditions. Seeing opportunities to help so many with this method, I decided to return to the United States.

My next assignment came through and everything fell into place. Before I knew it, I was establishing myself back in the Washington D.C. area. It felt good to get back to my familiar home, get my life settled in, and reconnect with friends and family. Immediately, I began sharing my new discovery and all of the successful healing work I had been doing. A few of them were willing to try it out on their own health issues. One longtime dear friend, a retired Army lieutenant colonel, had been struggling with hip, neck, and lower back pain. He had experienced a lot of stress in the transition from military to civilian life. Half way through the first session he said, "Wow, this is really amazing!" I asked, "Is something happening?" He replied, "Ah, yeah, it's like cool water washing down my back and over me. It's like all the tension is melting away with the water, going away from my head, neck, and back. I thought I was going to have to lie and tell you I felt great so I wouldn't hurt your feelings, but this really IS great!" After the treatment ended, he sent me a written testimonial:

I had great doctors and these doctors and their facilities had the best of resources. MRI, cortisone, hip scope, Celebrex and chiropractors. The best care money could buy. But I never got any relief from the pain. After receiving the treatment from you, I felt relaxed and calm, and the nagging hip pain I had for years went away. I had been seeing a chiropractor regularly and taking Celebrex for over four years. Following your treatment, in the course of a few days I ended both of these other forms of treatment. I will never, ever get another cortisone injection. Thank you.

These written testimonials continued to come in and motivated me to keep going and attend more training. After that, more doors opened. A new way and possibility of reaching people opened to me through the understanding of long-distance healing and group healing. Excited to test out the new knowledge of doing the treatments from a distance, I offered sessions to my great aunt, Jeanette, who lives in Maine. I let her know upfront that I had just learned this process and needed someone to test it out on to see how it would go. Jeannette is 86 years young, a woman who is full of life, and never afraid to speak her mind. I knew that if it didn't work, I could count on her being truthful. She nonchalantly agreed to the therapy, "Sure, I'll give it a try. The only thing I have to lose is my pain, why not?" With that, we set up the appointments.

In the course of this work, I found that older and elderly generations seem more receptive to this type of healing, more so than the people of my age group and those even younger. It appears that the older generation has either tried it all, has a feel for what does and doesn't work, or wise enough with experience to know that anything is possible.

Jeannette had debilitating, constant arthritis in both her hands and knees, and in both shoulders. Several years prior, her leg was amputated due to cancer. As a result, she had severe phantom pains, causing her to wake up all hours of the night screaming in agony. Phantom pains are excruciatingly painful sensations that people feel after having a limb or organ removed. They feel the pain as if the removed body part is still there, even though it is no longer physically a part of the body. However, as far as the energy body (otherwise called the aura or bio field) is concerned, energetically it is indeed very much still there, perhaps because the bio field informs the physical body. Some health professionals believe phantom pains are all psychological, but I would argue, what isn't? For the people who live with phantom pains, especially for years, the cause hardly matters, as the sensations are very real. The only thing that matters to the sufferer is how to fix it. Telling them it's all in their head doesn't help, especially if they aren't given tools to remedy the situation.

After the first distance session with Aunt Jeannette, she said, "I could definitely tell something was happening. My hands and shoulders got warm and I felt this tingling sensation in my body. I've never felt anything like that before! I'm bending my hands and the pain is mostly gone already. This is unbelievable Darcy! I can't wait for tomorrow!" Tomorrow came and she called me at the designated time. We chatted a few minutes about how she was feeling and how she slept really well through the night. One hand and shoulder felt really good, but she could feel lingering pain her knee and other shoulder and hand. I hung up the phone and went to work again, and twenty minutes later I phoned her back. She answered the phone, and before I could say anything she said, "Well you won't believe this, but something was really happening this time! I was rocking back and forth, and I thought to myself what am I doing that for? Then I realized there was tingling, but all the pain in my hands was gone. I'm bending them now and it's really gone! The real test will be when it rains in a few days, if the pain will come back or not," she said challengingly. "Let's see," I replied. "I expect a full report!"

The following days of remaining therapy were completed and over the next few weeks, she reported that the treatment resolved the pain in her shoulder, hands, and knee, and reduced her phantom pains. The severity and duration of each painful attack also lessoned in recurrence to one to two times a month, versus the almost nightly occurrences she had for the past several years. She let me know she was going to the doctor for a checkup and couldn't wait to tell her doctor about the results.

She called me after her appointment and said that the doctor was shocked to hear she was pain free, since she had been seeing Jeannette for several years and working to help her manage the pain. When Jeannette tried to tell the doctor more about the therapy, the doctor shut her down and wasn't interested in hearing about it. "If doctors are really interested in helping people, it makes you wonder why they wouldn't be interested in hearing about this?" she said pointedly. "Doctors aren't bad people," I said. "They just sometimes aren't aware of all the possibilities."

A couple more weeks passed and Aunt Jeannette called me again. "I have to tell you, Darcy, it rained almost all week and it didn't even bother me. There's still NO pain. I just can't believe it! All you did is call me on the phone and then somehow you did this. I can't imagine what you could possibly be doing all the way in Virginia." "It's hard to explain," I replied, not knowing where to begin. "Well, it doesn't matter to me anyway; all I know is I'm better!" She thanked me again for the treatments, and a few days later she sent me this testimonial:

When I was in my late 20s, early 30's, I was told that the pain in my hands was arthritis. I'm now 86 and have had arthritis in my hands, shoulders, and knee. Over the years, I have taken every new medication I heard of but without much help. A month ago Darcy called me and asked if I knew anything about energy healing. I had heard about some types of healing but really knew very little about it. She said, if I wanted her help, she would help me. I jumped at the chance. I had nothing to lose and the thought of living pain free sounded very good. We did twenty-minute sessions four days in a row, all from a distance. The first and second day, I had tingling and warmth in my hands and at the very tip of my fingers, by the fourth day the pain in my hands was gone. I was completely pain free and four to five weeks later I am still pain free. I am an amputee and have suffered with phantom pains for more than seven years; your treatment has helped greatly reduce that pain as well."

Performing this work illuminates how certain beliefs and frameworks in our society actually support and promote illness instead of wellness. The more people I came into contact with through this work, the more I recognized that the focus of one's personal philosophy of wellness is reflected in their state of health. Though I never noticed these things before, I began to connect the dots: thinking, beliefs and habits largely support the problems our society is trying desperately to overcome, especially in healthcare.

Looking around I noticed all the people hoping to make a difference by aligning themselves with awareness causes, walking, and running for Alzheimer's, Parkinson's, or breast cancer, that ubiquitous pink ribbon worn by so many. While all this attention may seem positive, it also increases awareness to illnesses that we want to avoid. Why focus on where we don't want to end up? The little pink ribbon is representing *dis-ease*. And if the pink ribbon isn't enough, we have an entire month dedicated to raising awareness of a cancer women want to avoid.

If we want something different, then we should carefully choose where we want to place our attention and intentions, discerning whether we will tap into the frequency of illness or the frequency of wellness. Why not change the message to "health and wellness awareness?" Let's tune our focus for more of what we want versus that which we don't want. It's clear that with the good nature of people, there's a desire to take action and do something for people who are suffering with illnesses. Focusing attention by creating a symbol like a pink ribbon that everyone now sees as breast cancer brings more energy to the problem side of the issue, thereby reinforcing it. Physically gathering for the fight of anything, or awareness of a problem, is a problem. Going to combat with them doesn't solve problems. We have compassion for the people living with these illnesses and we want to help them. We need to help them and reduce the number of instances of these occurrences in the future, but we do it by aligning to the solution. You get more health by focusing on more health. In other words, don't walk *for* breast cancer, walk *for* breast wellness! Gather in groups to talk about healthy habits in eating, exercise, living and reinforcing health, total well-being and useful living behaviors.

When we think about, talk about, and focus on a problem, we start to make space for the problem to continue in our consciousness, specifically, we are in accompaniment to it; like attracts like. Attention shapes how we live out our experiences. There's a well-known quote derived from the teachings of Lao Tzo:

"Watch your thoughts; they become words. Watch your words; they become actions. Watch your actions; they become habits. Watch your habits; they become character. Watch your character; it becomes your destiny."

This is not only about us as individuals, but also as a collective society. In society we can get addicted to talking about our problems, admiring them, and picking them apart. Problems and solutions, like illness and wellness exist at two different frequencies. Energy sets up materiality, and follows the path of least resistance, and as stated before, the Universe is a fair friend when it comes to your focus. Wherever you place your thoughts and emotions is the station we are tuning our frequency into and where the energy flows. It's one thing to think something, but when the heart gets on board with that thought or idea, the fire gets stoked and the amplification and intensity of that idea or activity really starts to get going. Pour more heart and desire behind an action and pretty soon the fire is blazing. This is where the magic unfolds, things really get rocking and momentum builds. Hopefully, it's momentum for what you want. When an entire society starts a movement with its hearts and minds, the result can be an unstoppable force — it is how governments are overthrown, and new ones are created. When more than one-person starts thinking and feeling passionate about a solution, a group dynamic is created, making that group extremely powerful. The law of resonance says that when collections of potentials are together, eventually they will all become synchronized to the highest potential. A cited example is when a house full of women eventually have synchronized menstrual cycles. Another example is grandfather clocks lined up against a wall, with swinging pendulums. Eventually, synchronization occurs with the swing.

Nature works on this principle, which is one reason why group dynamics within organizations are so important and interesting. If you have ever been involved in a group, you probably have noticed that after a couple of days, the group dynamics begin to evolve. Depending on the type of group and the personalities involved, the results can be either beautiful or disturbing. Healing focused groups can have amazing results if the group dynamics are properly seen to.

I experienced more exposure to group dynamics by working under Zoran's guidance as he led his healing clinics. Each time I worked with him, there was a noticeable boost in my own health and spiritual evolution. After watching 25 to 35 people heal at a time, and spending a couple hours each day for four days in a room chock-full of energy, I felt the impact. Each time, those experiences changed me and, at times, it took me months to fully comprehend what had transpired.

Zoran makes it look easy because he is an expert maestro at orchestrating the flow of a large group at healing events. The success or failure within something like this lies in the leader's understanding and ability to lead the group in a way that keeps the focus on the intended outcome: wellness. When a group of people show up for healing, the intentions are set. Fundamentally, the leader of the group is the highest potential holding the focus of health. As the event is beautifully orchestrated, promoting only wellness, reinforcing happy and healthy behaviors and interactions, the participants can't help but become well. These types of healing groups are genius because they also affect people on an unconscious level. Not only are those attending affected because they are sitting amongst the energy of wellness, but they are also observing and watching major healing unfold with the other members of the group right before their eyes. Changes are being observed, even unconsciously, which create healing on the subconscious level.

After watching the healings occur over and over again I started to think more about society as a whole. What behaviors do people's intentions and thoughts reinforce? If we heal this way, shifting our attention on wellness, what else could we solve by focusing in a different way?

The same holds true for activists who are passionate about their causes. As soon as someone stands up to fight against "insert anything," they have actually come into energetic alignment with what they are fighting. Fighting against anything is still a focus of energy, and, essentially, more power to it. Activists have beautiful hearts for change, but often the focus is just a few degrees off. To really see a shift in a society, country, and, indeed, the world, there must be a collective shift in focus. Mother Teresa understood this concept very well. She said, "I was once asked why I don't participate in anti-war demonstrations. I said that I will never do that, but as soon as you have a pro-peace rally, I'll be there." We have to peace for peace.

When our inner worlds are at peace, our need for fighting will be eliminated from our external human experience. When knowledge of who we are is known from the inside, evidence of that fact is visible on the outside; there is nothing left to fight for or against.

When more people focus on being in alignment and acceptance of who they truly are, thinking and doing not just for themselves but for each other, the more they become the change they want and expect to see. We must all begin with ourselves in order to see a more harmonious outcome created for our society. Random acts of kindness and radical acts of forgiveness happening individually build momentum for change on multiple levels, bleeding over to families, communities, and so on.

It is not so much about being a problem solver as it is about being a solution promoter. We could start by admiring the solutions that empower more love, joy, and passion instead of the problems in our own life and see how personal change could be experienced. Try stoking a different fire with our thoughts, emotions, and activities. Resolve personal conflicts, internally and externally; we don't always have to go to every argument or fight that we are invited to, we always have a choice.

Our implicit agreement is what holds up the framework as it is. Our participation is the only thing that makes existence of anything possible, regardless if we are for or against. There *is* good happening in this world, it is happening all around us if we take the time to acknowledge it. It's not just bad in our communities and around the world. Good news is rarely reported as much as the dramatic, fearful, and traumatic stories of the world. We can keep up with world events without entrenching ourselves in the gory details and being consumed with the fear and negativity of it all. Support publications that talk about positive things that interest you, good news stories that inspire joy, passion and creativity in society.

This is more than wishful thinking and prayer alone. The groundwork for wellness and peace start with individual thoughts and behaviors, with the way we treat each other and ourselves. The seemingly small acts create a new life cadence, which is felt throughout communities and eventually becomes a collective consciousness of society. Buildings don't just appear; they are built on foundations, one brick at a time.

CHAPTER 13

A Healer's Journey

"The soul always knows what to do to heal itself. The challenge is to silence the mind."

— Caroline Myss

Initially, I was resistant to being called a healer. This was new and uncharted territory for me. In order to be taken seriously, would I have to conform to the public perception of what healers looked like? I saw myself as quite different from those who fell into this category. In my mind, there was no getting me into that box.

There was this notion of having to be "all-in." In most cases, that meant an office, website, business cards, and a nice fancy portrait, even some healer-like clothes made from purple hemp or something. After all, the more spiritual I looked the more people would regard me as a great healer, right? Yet the exterior trappings were not important and had nothing to do with being an effective healer. The key for me was just to go out and do the work; set an intention to help as many others heal and the rest flows and naturally follows. That other stuff was irrelevant.

The longer I did the healing work, the more I realized that quitting my day job was not an option. There are many great healers making a living from doing healing work. I knew that. I also knew that I was following my heart in learning the work, but needed time to evaluate my intentions and motivation for pursuing healing because I knew that realization would be critical to the healing process itself.

While helping others to heal is a great honor, before I could help humanity, I had to first help myself. There were some steps missing. I was still learning to integrate gratitude and humility into my healing work. I had met so many other healers who took themselves too seriously, and I didn't want that for myself. After the lessons I received in gratitude and humility, I needed to be patient and believe that things would happen according to the divine timing. I really needed to make peace with that, and slowly and eventually I did.

Much like other paradoxes in life, the more I learned the less I really knew. Everything I once believed was now different, or proved untrue. There were a lot of other things that I didn't know as well. Being a healer is as much of a lesson for the healer as it is for the client; both remember to trust the process, the process of life. This also meant that I had to make sure that, as the healer, I stayed out of the way of other people's healing process. Gaining that insight brought comfort to being called a healer because all I really had to do was hold the space of wellness, the rest I decided, was always up to my clients.

In the beginning, I thought I wanted to do this work full time. At that stage, it wouldn't have worked for me because I wasn't ready. I was still in the process of so much transformation and healing myself, still undergoing a major deconstruction and expansion of the new me that I was now claiming. However, I was burning the candle at both ends, running hard day and night, trying to build something that I hadn't even stopped to ask myself if it was what I really wanted.

The fun thing about becoming aware of energy is that when you have things to resolve, you will recognize the theme of it popping into your life in a bunch of different ways until you face it. Doing healing work teaches, and somehow it always led me to clients that brought those unresolved themes to me, scratching the surface of issues that pushed my buttons over and over again, until I learned the lessons.

At that time, I wasn't ready to deal with the public full time, and thankfully didn't take the leap. I still needed to learn to find peace and balance with my work and home life. Jumping into a startup business would only have thrusted me into a chaotic tailspin.

I was living in the D.C. area at the time and working at the Pentagon. I was coming home in the evenings and working with three or four clients a night. It was the most I could do; all that I really needed.

Setting up a full time business didn't turn out necessary. The people I came into contact with every day, even at work, were my community. If I was really talking about being of service, then the people I interacted with on a daily basis were my community. The UPS man, the person who sold me my coffee, my administrative assistant, and my neighbors were all my community. The greatest transformations first start within small communities. It only takes a couple of well-intentioned, determined and service-minded individuals to be change agents. I learned not to underestimate the effectiveness of a single person's ability to lift, support, and heal a magnitude of people. The more exposure I have to this work, and having met others doing similar work, the more I see the great impact one person can have.

Nevertheless, I've met many healers along the way who shared the same vision I first had of starting this huge business with an office space, all the advertising and the business cards. There's nothing wrong with building such a business, but I realized that the best way for the healing work to function for me was to keep it simple and to help one person at a time.

As I work with clients today, I never know how they will be affected or what their outcome will be. People come for all sorts of reasons and their journey is what's important. I'm just holding space. My deepest, most profound, and life-changing healing experiences as a healer were experienced with the people in my immediate circle or one degree away. That's where it started for me, being of service with the people I knew. The native Indians believed that every family and community had a healer. I started with the people in my family and then expanded to the people in my neighborhood, at the grocery store, and in the park. The people I didn't know found me through the people I did know and who I had helped, and from there it continues to grow. All people are people worth helping; everyone can benefit from healing on some level.

The results of my influence in my immediate circle could be seen in a short period of a few months. More people were healed in my community than I ever could have touched had I just gone directly to open a standard healing practice. Spending tons of money on marketing and advertising, sitting someplace waiting and hoping for people to walk through the door, that wouldn't have worked for me. My everyday community of people trusts me to help them because they know me, we have rapport. They hear the honesty and passion in my words when they listen to me speak about the things I've seen and done with my own two hands. By working in my community, new options of wellness are brought to the group where there is already an established level of trust.

People still ask if I do this work full time. Sometimes that question is said in a challenging way, implying that my success level is directly tied to how many hours I work. I've learned and cultivated a skill to help people heal. I like what I do as a healer, but I also enjoy being around regular everyday people with everyday lives who don't come to me for healing. I don't feel a need to segregate myself from the mainstream. I'm not here to hide away in an enclave or subculture of people quietly only doing healing work. I'm here to go mainstream and share messages of love, forgiveness, inspiration and acceptance with the world, and healing work is just one way to relay a message.

I've been known, and known myself, as many things: a mother, daughter, sister, a career-minded woman, and an Army veteran who also happens to know how to be a healer. That's the integrity of the situation, even though it probably sounds really common, and maybe not that compelling.

Possibly, it sounds less spiritual too. I don't know how to sound more, or be more spiritual, than I already am. As if being a spirit in the human form isn't spiritual enough. There are no frills, no ego show. It's just helping people to remember who they truly are, with me as the messenger delivering a bit of information in a divine meeting, arranged by the Universe.

CHAPTER 14

Warrior's Rest

"Warriors are not what you think of as warriors. The Warrior is not someone who fights, because no one has the right to take another life. The Warrior, for us is one who sacrifices self for the good of others. Their task is to take care of the elderly, the defenseless, those who cannot provide for themselves, and above all the children, the future of humanity."

— Sitting Bull,
Warrior Wisdom: the heart and soul of Bushido

There was once a tradition among Native American warriors, who would undergo a period of rest and attend to mental, emotional, and even physical wounds. They would rest to let aspects of life integrate and make peace with the things they had endured, essentially taking their time to focus internally. This cleansing period served as a way to avoid bringing the energy of violence and disorder of battles back to the tribe. Even warriors need rest and relaxation in order to keep their balance and return to peace. With support from their tribal members and Shaman (tribal healer), the warriors allowed themselves time to work through and feel any issues that arose in this process. Some also did this process with a ceremony. This was a period of reflection, respect, and reconnection with themselves. As a result, these warriors were able to reclaim their inner balance. Once they had rested and rediscovered their balance of life, they would rejoin the tribal society. They understood the importance of taking care of themselves first, so that they could better take care of others in the tribe that depended on them for support.

I felt like a warrior who needed to rest. Professionally, I was still working full-time while also promoting my healing work. Personally, I was also in a serious relationship, my daughter was transitioning to her first year of college, and my mother was diagnosed with breast cancer. Not sleeping enough or taking any days off, I hit a wall. In an attempt to do everything, be everything to everyone, I was becoming more and more disconnected from that feeling of inner balance I gained from doing the healing work. I was starting to feel resentful of the people in my life that wanted more of my time and resentful about staying in my day job. New clients had almost completely stopped calling me for treatments and it confused me at the time. As that was happening, my romantic relationship fell apart at the seams. I reached another juncture of my life where I was being forced to take another look at myself and press the reset button on a number of things. Once again, the cyclical nature of life was coming around and caught up with me in a Universal, divine order kind of way. It wasn't like a gracious little cherub nudging me to slow down, be kinder and more forgiving to others and myself for transgressions of the present and past either. It was more like a cosmic bitch slap that occurs in the most beautifully orchestrated series of life disasters, forcing me to stop everything and take a complete inventory of what I was doing and how I was living. What can I say? Sometimes it takes me a few iterations of the lesson to get the point. Life's lessons always show up for me as needed, until the point is taken, and this time would be no exception.

I needed to push pause on everything and everyone in my life. No more commitments could be made; I needed to commit to me. It takes courage to stop everything, and I mean every single thing you are doing that involves a commitment. Cut away all those little projects and busy things that you are chasing and maintaining and just *be* with you. A warrior's rest seems simple, yet many people either overlook the importance of stopping for a period of time or are terrified to do it. I mean really do it. Really doing it means stop calling friends when bored. Stop endless texting and hours of social media perusing. Stop eating and drinking out of boredom, shopping, excessive exercising and even the spiritual busy work and endless rituals that are created to make you feel productive and on your path. Stop everything, just stop, and stop it right now. Can you imagine it? What does the thought of that do to you? Would you feel alone, or worse, lonely? What emotions or things that need to be faced come for you when you aren't busy avoiding them and have nothing else to do? Can you just sit, be, and experience that solitude without running away from yourself? It's not easy.

All those questions came forward for me as I stopped everything. When first beginning this period of quietness,

I was riddled with an anxiety that kept me wanting to forge forward and find something new to do. For years I had been distracting myself with emotional busy work in relationships, spiritual busywork disguised as self-help "programs," learning and doing an unhealthy amount of healing work for others, while also attempting to be the help desk for everyone else's life problems around me.

As an avid list creator, I lived to check off completed tasks. I was a task-oriented, productive mamma-jammer. If I wasn't checking blocks, I felt an insistent nagging feeling like I should be accomplishing something, being proactive toward a task in some way, just doing something, anything at all really.

I remember times when stillness came knocking and it terrified me. Coming back from Iraq, any period of inactivity would toss me into a full on anxiety and panic attack. I had developed the habit of pushing myself to stay constantly busy for the sake of not stopping. My bosses loved me. I was the most productive person an organization could ask for. When things slowed down, I had this internal sensor that would suddenly and feverishly say, "Quick, find a productive distraction!" If there wasn't any work, I would invent some and rush around trying to achieve the next big goal or look for the next external thing that would somehow distract or attempt to fulfill me. This was the way I avoided facing difficult emotions. Years were spent in this erratic ebb and flow. It was a self-created sense of urgency. While in Europe, I saw the drivers of this behavior ran much deeper. This was avoidance. Friends and family used to say that I was "motivated," "productive," and "high achieving." Really, I was just scared to stop moving because on the inside I knew if I did, I would be forced to face what was quietly brewing deep down—my heart—and that was incredibly scary to face.

The day came when enough was enough. I was exhausted from myself. There was nothing left to do but stop and face the difficult things that I had successfully avoided for most of my journey. Stopping everything and sitting in silence was a daunting thing. All the masks fell off in the ultimate face-off between me, myself, and I. We are sometimes different people when we are alone than when interacting with others. There was no one there to impress and no expectation of whom I had to be. All the pretenses transmuted, and it was an experience of total realness, taking time to observe nothing but the rawness of me, the very simple essence of myself.

I was no longer playing traffic cop or air traffic controller, submerging myself in other people's problems in an attempt to avoid mine or make them go away. Sitting in my chair day after day, I contemplated what was just being. It sounds like a weird riddle, aren't we all still doing something by "being?" Yes, we are, but unlike everything else, it is the only thing that we are required to actually do. As a result, not long after, doing nothing became okay and easy for me. In my space of "being" there was comprehension that I was actually doing so much more than I ever imagined. It became okay to observe and even sink into the moments of solitude, and enjoy being with myself in silence. None of it happened without first fully surrendering to the madness and chaos that ensued inside of me. Once I surrendered, with the taking of a deep breath, the long pause afterwards became the most healing thing I've ever done for myself. I grew curious as to why I was so drawn to this epic solitude now, at this point in my life. I was never clear about the answer, I just *was*, and that became good enough for me. Of all the places visited and traveled around the world and all the things I have done, this journey inward has been the one that has taught me the most.

This type of solitude is about taking time to be kinder, and to love, honor, and honestly recognize myself. We hear about this all the time. Everyone talks about loving yourself and loving your life, work, and family. Everyone nods their head up and down, but do we know what it means to truly love ourselves? I remember hearing that throughout the years and thinking, "Yeah, of course I love myself." But then wondering, how exactly are you supposed to love yourself? What does it really mean? Isn't it easier just to find someone else to love you? I didn't really get it. I was never able to quantify or fully understand so I just went on with life and to my next distraction, as I think most people do.

Loving yourself means first making a commitment to you. Vowing to love yourself for better or worse, even relentlessly staying by your own side, no matter what. Not just during the good times, but even when you make bad choices or screw things up, even with the cellulite on your thighs and all. This love has to occur before you can attempt to love anyone else.

It can be complicated because love means different things to different people. The word love is layered with meaning and feathered with convoluted understanding. Love is just another word or idea until you put it to an action, and then it becomes something easier to see as

223

real. It's like when love is applied to something, it can make it more understandable and tangible. A warrior's rest is self-love in the action of *Be*-ing. *Be*ing is the acknowledgement of your true self. When making a real effort to dedicate a significant amount of time to *Be*-ing; taking a pause in life, listening in to the stillness of your soul, you do begin to feel the sense of alignment and hear a soft whisper of all that's needed speaking to you. Some people will probably read this and think that I'm saying stop and meditate. Or take time for yourself to do nothing, to just read a book or watch T.V. That's not doing nothing, that's still doing something and it's another distraction. I didn't meditate at all during this period because that was something else I would be doing a certain way, obsessively grading myself on how well I performed it. The last thing I needed was another task to master. Meditation is good. In fact, it's better than good—it's *great*. But what I'm talking about is just sitting and *Be*-ing with absolutely no framework to follow, no real instructions, and nothing to do. Some people could characterize what I'm saying as being lazy, and most likely social conditioning will have to be set aside in order to really appreciate being able to do absolutely nothing. If you were with someone who was in dire need of love, compassion, and comfort, giving your total presence and attention to them would be called an act of love. I needed to love myself in that same way, and still often do.

Taking time to be with you, really being present with acknowledgement of your true self is fulfilling the commitment to be the person you can count on and trust. It's the first thing that needs to happen, before you can commit externally to anyone else. By doing so, you are giving the priority inward and paying attention to the soft voice of intuition that probably has something to tell you.

Things came up, oh, and didn't they come up! One by one, and there was plenty seen that I didn't like about myself. Things I wasn't proud of, things that made me laugh, and things that made me cry, sometimes at the same time. I watched my insecurities and fears bubble to the surface, recognizing and observing the harshness and judgment I used to answer those insecurities and fears. Hearing how crassly and judgmentally my inner voice sounded made me cringe. I also recognized that I judged and compared what I considered were my inadequacies to the adequacies of others. Many facets of my human self and ego came forward to play, including the behaviors that embarrassed me; my vindictiveness, meanness, my scary and selfish self. I saw the ego that was so judgmental and fearful. There was also a compassionate one with tender-loving honesty and passion. There was the kind up-lifter and encourager, the inspirer and the one with so much integrity and honor. With that, I realized it's all the same heart; the good and the bad, however the good and bad are defined. My judgments and criticism were seen in a new light. Observing myself, I realized that, more often than not, the things I said to others were the exact things I needed to hear most myself. It was hard to work through some of these realizations in the period of solitude. The remedy, I knew, was all about love, acceptance and recognition for my true self, in a different way than I had considered before. My understanding of what it really means to love oneself expanded to another level. Even looking at all the things

I perceived negatively, there was perfection within those imperfections; another paradox that resides in us all. How perfectly flawed every one of us truly is, and the divine perfection of all that is (flaws and all).

There were many realizations about how my life was being lived that bubbled to the surface. Relationships had always been a big challenge for me. When everything around me stopped, I was able to gain clarity on a pattern in my love life. As a result, I made a commitment to take a break from relationships. As all this was happening, a previous boyfriend and now a dear friend for many years reentered my life briefly. He was my sounding board and go-to guy for all things that required understanding and sanity checking. We dated others over the years and somehow we always stayed supportive of each other and came back around; a constant and supportive friendship. One day he didn't come back though. The thing I always suspected would happen one day did and I knew it was best for him. He found someone else and maintaining a close friendship with me was no longer okay. It was difficult to deal with at first because he had been my anchor and sense of safety in the past. He was the one who told me I was all right whenever I panicked. I trusted his judgment so when he told me everything was all right, in my world it was. However, in my time of solitude, I knew that being in any kind of relationship—even just a friendship—he would need things of me in return. Things that I had no bandwidth to give him, but that he really deserved. I had to let him go, and as hard as it was, for the first time in many years, I felt truly liberated of any obligations of my heart. Relying on the friendship as I had took up emotional space and created codependency for me in a fashion that I hadn't realized in the past.

I spent a lot of time in quietness, facing all of these unresolved situations that were now showing up to have their big moment of reckoning. The biggest part of this process for me was learning to listen to the information without judgment (either of others or myself) and allowing whatever emotion or experience to arise as needed, and then being able to forgive myself, forgive the others involved, and then just let it go; LET.IT.GO became my mantra.

It's amazing what you are able to hear when the internal judgmental chatter and endless questioning cease. It was not only an exercise of surrender, but also of trust. Today, I still find it helpful to take time every day to sit and just be in the present moment. These days, I'm a lot more peaceful internally, and starting my day in a peaceful way sets the tone.

I'm still a human and life still shows up with its share of problems like anyone else, but having this peaceful resolution process allows me to face things nimbly and move on with an open heart.

CHAPTER 15

Dark Night of the Soul

"You wander from room to room, hunting for the diamond necklace that is already around your neck."
— Rumi

There was a sixteenth-century Spanish poet and Roman Catholic Mystic, St. John of the Cross, who wrote *"La noche oscura del alma"* (Dark Night of the Soul). The poem explains how periods of darkness can speak to the adversities in one's life. These can be painful or troublesome times, in which a seeking soul pursues relief from the burdens of life's dark moments by connecting with the Creator, Universe or God. The poem talks about the painful emotional crisis that people endure as they seek to unearth spiritual maturity. It's a term that represents a spiritual crisis. For hundreds of years, this subject has been mulled over by great poets, philosophers, and others, including F. Scott Fitzgerald, who, in his 1945 collection of essays, "The Crack Up[10],"

---

[10] Fitzgerald, F. (1956). *The crack-up, with other uncollected pieces, notebooks and unpublished letters; together with letters to Fitzgerald from*

said, "In the real dark night of the soul it is always three o'clock in the morning." I guess he understood the quiet stillness and solitude of that hour and the deep solemnness of contemplation that can be had right before the sun rises and the bustle of life overtakes us. My period of rest and surrender felt like a dark night of soul, and it was crucial for me in order to move forward. It almost felt like the deep dark pause was a rite of passage in my evolution in order to process all the changes and transitions taking place in my life.

Changes can be described as the shifts—which may or may not be within our control—that happen physically and externally in a situation. Transitions are the internal psychological and emotional reorientation process that can occur in response to a change. A metamorphosis within us unfolds with the integration of changes and transitions.

My dear friend, Sandy, often uses a well-known quote to describe change: "It isn't the changes that do us in, it's the transitions." The saying suggests that a change isn't nearly the impactful complication as the transition that touches off the emotional and psychological impacts, following or preceding the external shift. She is a seasoned veteran on the art of navigating the difficulties of changes and transitions. After her divorce she did a complete lifestyle redesign, which began with the decision to sell the residence she lived in for over 20 years. Her youngest child leaving for college at the end of the summer preceded this decision. There were some new career opportunities and professional endeavors that were lying ahead as well

Gertrude Stein, Edith Wharton, T.S. Eliot, Thomas Wolfe, and John Dos Passos; and essays and poems. New York: [J. Laughlin].

and she needed to be lighter to pursue them. I spent a number of days with her in the home where she had lived and raised her children, discussing and walking through how the transition would take place. We went through each room systematically, and began rolling away two decades of bags and boxes to discard. Acting as her transition coach, my job was to support her as she moved toward her goal. Even the most seasoned athletes have coaches, and she was wise enough to know that support would be helpful to her throughout this life changing process. As an objective party to the situation, I had no emotional investment to the history of things that were about to be sold or given away to charity. My involvement was to anchor her desired result throughout the process, and help her make sense of what to keep within pragmatic reason.

Navigation of life shifts can be taxing, and it is always helpful to have a sounding board during this type of conversion. Bringing in nonpartisan assistance helped with Sandy's decision process as she emotionally and physically broke up with the life she once had. It was a challenge, there was 20 plus years' worth of stuff to go through; several closets, rooms, and drawers were filled with items and memories of her life's past. She had tough but logical decisions to make over those days about what to keep and what to dump as she downsized and simplified her life. The remaining items would leave her lighter while generating the shape of her new life. What would the resulting change look like in the end? Emotionally and physically, this process was heavy and exhausting. Doing new things can be scary and tiresome and this life-changing ordeal was no exception. When we reached the end of the third day of sorting, trash cans were bursting at the seams as they waited to be picked up on the side of the road, and several more bags and boxes were dropped off to the local charity center.

By the end of the thinning-out process of her life possessions, she was left feeling weightless and more mobile. This too is a type of emotional surrender and release. After the process was complete she had a new sense of freedom and realization about how ready she had been to move on. Most of all, completing this process gave her the necessary closure for ending a chapter in her life, while constructing an open palette for the beginning of a new and exciting chapter. It's important to note that results can be achieved using various approaches. Some people have to sit in silence, and others can find release and surrender in other ways. The approach that resonates best for the individual is what should be adopted.

When my life activities resumed after my dark rest, it felt like I had excavated many old thoughts and behaviors as well, and as a result I felt better equipped and emotionally renewed, like I was stepping into a new version of myself. My zest and passion for the odyssey was reborn. I was excited about my future, but in a different way. I felt the excitement intensely, but I also felt myself settling into a new sense of assurance that everything unfolds as it should for me in due time.

Over the years, it seemed that with every transition I made there was also an evolution taking place within me. I was systematically shedding the old while ushering in the new, whether that concerned friends, relationships, unproductive situations, illness, old beliefs, or thought processes. Each time, it felt like I was going through a deliberate, and sometimes painful, death. Sometimes that process was easy, and sometimes it was not so easy. How difficult it was depended on my thinking, how much I tried to control the outcome, or how high the perceived stakes were for the outcome. As painful and difficult as it was for me to let things go, it needed to be done in order to make space for something else to emerge and be born.

Death and birth can be painful processes, but without either the circle of life wouldn't continue. Sometimes I hear people talk about their life and they'll speak about their younger years and say, "That was another lifetime." Even though it's still the same lifetime, that period was another time of their lives. It's a significant statement because they're recognizing that they have had closure on that part of their lives and made a transition to a new period. To me that is what is important, that we be willing to let things go, and that we are always willing to update our opinions and stances in our lives. Life is meant to evolve, be lived fluidly and with movement, always flowing like a boundless river, not stagnant and still like a contained body of pond water.

In the process of letting go of what did not serve or align with my new vision, I found an energetic revival was created. A gust of new and fresh life rushed through the front door. There's tremendous energy flow that gets created when we start letting go of stuff, whether it's an old dress we intended to wear several years ago and still never have, or a thought process that monopolizes us, mentally and emotionally. Consciously releasing clears the clutter, creating room for something new to come in.

In life, it seems like everything is constantly updating, reconfirming, and recreating itself. It reminds me of the

Ouroboros, the ancient Greek symbol depicting the serpent devouring its own tail. It signifies the cyclical nature of things, how everything is constantly recreating itself. To me, it eludes that if everything is cyclical in nature, as with any circular entity, there is no ending or beginning.

If there is no ending and beginning then there are just reiterations, updated versions of the same, but filtered with new eyes, framing, and higher perspectives. So maybe life is the constant, maybe it itself doesn't change. Instead, we change and each time we go around, our views, perceptions, and thoughts are updated, constantly recreating things to be seen from a new and higher perspective. *We* are what is constantly changing and transitioning.

Of course there was doubt that existed inside of me each time there was a major life change or leap to something else. If I looked calm and cool on the outside, like a duck gliding across the surface of a lake, be sure I was indeed paddling like heck below the surface to get to the other side of the transition. It's natural to have some internal struggle when experiencing anything new, especially when you don't have a clear idea of what might come from the transition in the end, or the confidence of past performance to lean on. We never know how things can turn out until we do it by learning how to persevere in faith and courage ourselves. We can begin to have faith that whatever shows up in life is there to help, not sabotage, our process. When charting an unknown course, uncertainty and fear will always exist on some level in the back of our minds. I think it comes down to knowing that there's a choice to be made, either we use doubt and fear to be our motivation charging us forward, or we let it immobilize us, getting

233

stuck in a loop of uncertainty. Most new things in life will seem uncertain in the beginning. If we wait for the whole path to be illuminated and glowing with certainty, there would be no forward movement and nothing would ever get accomplished. We have to be willing to put a stake in the ground at some point and go for it. Each transition point in my life was a blind walk of faith. I never really knew how things would work out for certain; I was guessing, testing, and trying to listen to my intuition, hoping it was the best choice. Sometimes it was, and sometimes it wasn't. As a result, today I barely recognize the girl who once lived in that small town in Maine. Indeed, that was another lifetime.

In our heart and soul we always seem to know when a change is coming or needed. The head may disagree because it has an investment in a position or station to defend, but the heart always knows—after all, we are much more than a mind that is thinking. Thinking can be easily hacked, maneuvered, and manipulated with word games and fast talkers; these are carnival tricks, not mastery of life. It's more difficult, if not impossible, to hack the true song of one's tuned-in heart and inherent intuition. This is because we are a soul behind the thinking mind; the mind is just the tip of the iceberg, and the remaining two-thirds of us are not easily seen from the surface. The heart and soul are leaders of truth and passion for a world we all desire and deserve to live in. This is about flexibility, creation, and fluidity within the spiritual intellect of human evolution.

Mind constructs are powerful, as noted in examples in the previous chapters. We may want to consider the many ways to move beyond, in keeping the status quo, we empower these constructs by continuing to participate and play with them. They can be easily identified for yourself by the way it feels in your body if you stop, feel, and listen. The difference is that the head games of consciousness do not feel good in the body. Understanding in the heart and soul can also be felt by slowing down and unplugging from life, even if it's just for 15 minutes a day. This is the experience and intelligence we are born with; this is how we access our knowing from within. Over time, when we don't listen to the indications that come with a sensation in our body we build little conflicts within us. Maybe we ignore that sinking feeling in the pit of our stomachs when something isn't right, or the small flutter in our heart when something is. These conflicts can affect us in many ways, sometimes translating to life chaos and illnesses either in our physical or emotional states of being. Finding ways to listen to the indicators of the heart pulls our personal empowerment lever, which supports our highest knowing of who we are, in our genuine *be*-ing. When we are able to do that, we access the inner voice of our knowing, which is also aligned with the balance of nature.

In this period of rest and reflection, I discovered that I had been doing everything in my life based on my belief for survival. Decisions were made in order to keep climbing the ladder to success and professional security. In relationships, I had reduced my vulnerability and exposure by choosing men who would never fully choose me back either. This need for creating protection and security from exposure was all in my mind. Doing these personal risk assessments kept me from fully committing to anyone. So relationships became touch and go, disappointing and disastrous.

235

Next, I chose a career that I thought would never let me down. It kept me busy, always employed, always with a new adventure. Besides climbing the professional ladder, I was also protecting myself. Let's face it, dealing with a computer is much less complex than dealing with a human.

Protecting myself from ever being vulnerable is an interesting concept in correlation to my professional vocation of remediating vulnerability on complex computer systems. In the external things all around us, there are always clues to lead us to what needs to be discovered from within us most. I needed to find and face that same vulnerability on the inside that I was so good at identifying on the outside, and be willing to walk through it no matter how uncomfortable it felt.

On the other side of that vulnerability was my true self; the perfection and imperfections, all the things that made me who I was. Being genuine isn't about perfection; it is about learning to stand in the truth of who we are without apology or concession. To me, it is about showing up and embodying our message, or our purpose in our unique way.

It is heart-guided living, and allows you to stand anywhere as who you are, regardless of where you are, be it Iraq or the local Wal-Mart. It doesn't mean I don't feel the energy of chaos and disorder of those places when there. It's noticed, and still I'm standing in the truth of who I am. Whatever it is, is fine with me either way, but I'm never fighting it, or in fear of it, I'm just *be*-ing.

CHAPTER 16

My Human Experience

"I looked in temples, churches and mosques. But I found the Divine within my heart."

— Rumi

The totality of who we are is more than our thoughts, beliefs, and actions. Those expressions are surface fragments of the infinite expressional capability of our spiritual selves. Our physical existence is tethered to our preeminent spiritual being, our greater essence. Hints of this existence have been noted by many as the soft voice inside, the spark of light from within that brings us through in dark and destitute moments, or even as the Holy Spirit.

Our greater essence is the immaterial entity of our whole being; it's our spirit. Since it is a part of the total sum of who we are, everything we do is spiritual work. Even living out our daily lives—regardless of whether we perceive our lives as mundane or daring adventures of epic proportions. The greater essence is consistent and ever-present. It doesn't make mistakes or take wrong turns.

It doesn't recognize choices made on alternate paths as misguided decisions. It sees every decision and path as an opportunity to explore a new realm of understanding within the human experience.

The dynamics of humans are gloriously complex and rich, and ever-sought after by the evolving greater essence of our beings. With doing comes learning, a timeless and universal truth. Evolution at any level is born out of experience. I believe the spirit chooses the human form, and earth is our spiritual university. Being human facilitates contrast and provides context and definition for life. If there were only one way to live, resulting in one way of being, what kind of human experience would that be?

Throughout life so far, I've learned that we can choose many different ways of living. None of it is wrong or right, it's just merely what we pick or don't pick. Since the way I chose was based upon my personal history, education, and past experiences, I became careful about giving advice to others. While my beliefs lined up with what I know and have done, someone else might come away with a completely different assessment.

Even with those close to me, I'm mindful of the advice given. My daughter is a successful, ambitious, and career-minded young woman who has been working in the dental field as a hygienist. She now finds herself at a major crossroads. Should she be content with her present position, continue her education towards becoming a dentist, or become an educator in the field of dentistry? We often discuss the options ahead of her and I always end the conversation with the same advice. "All options are good options," I tell her. "You can't make a mistake no matter what you choose. If you don't like it, you can make a new choice to do something else. No one can make the choice but you. This life is in your hands."

I truly believe that whatever she does, she will continue her great journey with interest and passion for the endeavor. Even as a parent, I perceive that my role has to be more consulting in life decisions, because she is on her own path of discovery. I work hard within myself to deconstruct my fears as I sometimes see her doing things that could be considered undesirable. When I see her floundering, unable to make choices, I remind myself that I bounced around the world (literally) for years while trying to figure out my life. The fears my parents must have felt were probably much larger than anything my own parental experience has given me.

We all reach certain checkpoints in life that require us to figure things out. With each checkpoint we cross through and the decisions we make, we begin to learn who we truly are and what we are capable of doing. If someone else is always making the decisions for us, always driving us around in our stagecoach of life, we never evolve or learn how to go at it alone or independently. If we never get the reigns in our own hands, we aren't doing what we are here to do: evolve our essence. We miss learning how to make our perceptions possible; ultimately we never own our potency. It takes courage to take a leap of faith with only an idea or a vision. By doing so, it means we have to begin walking before the path is actually below our feet, and owning the outcome. If that experience isn't a spiritual one, I don't know what is. The human logical mind would never agree to begin walking where there is no ground below. The spirit, the higher order of consciousness says, "Walk and I will show up for you, I promise."

Our essence is constantly reminding us, however gently or fiercely, to remember the sanctity of the human existence. The question is, do we ever put it together? I don't believe the perfection of our existence means we live in a zero defects bubble, safely and quietly flying below the radar undetected, sliding through life without ever having a broken heart, making a mess, or living through difficulties. There were times that I made a mess in my life. But, if given the chance, I wouldn't have done it any differently because, by my estimation, all of my past experiences have brought me to understanding of who I am today.

I have learned something from everyone in my life—my daughter, cab drivers, coworkers, and the cashier where I buy my groceries. Layers of learning are there, shaping who we are in every interaction with the people around us if we choose to see them. As an experiment, I deliberately became more cognizant of ways of interacting and responding to people in pain or experiencing difficult times. Intently listening, pausing my need to think or prepare to respond, I made an effort to see their position or point of view. With that it was easier to observe and respond to people in a light of love, compassion, and understanding. People need more compassion and understanding no matter where they are in life.

Essentially, I always attempt to connect with each person's essence, the light that shines through them. It could be considered a light of oneness or our divinity. There are plenty of people who are more qualified to speak on oneness. I don't consider myself a teacher of oneness, but am deeply aware of the connectedness existing between all things. This ever-present essence, which connects us and resides within us all, is often missed in our daily interactions with each other because we get so caught up and consumed in our own life processes.

Every eulogy I've ever heard or obituary I've ever read always says the same kind of thing. People remember what kind of person the deceased was, not what material things they attained or how many bonuses they received as a successful CEO. People talk about the person's acts of kindness, meaningful contributions made to their family, their community, and society. They discuss the nature of the person's heart and soul, remembering the goodness and how he or she affected the lives left behind on earth. The reflection is on the person's soul, grace and goodness, the light of oneness. Why do we wait for someone to die before acknowledging and celebrating his or her essence? What if we attempted to acknowledge the goodness of everyone's light each day, even if it is just one tiny aspect?

When realizations of spirituality and oneness started coming at me, it was like I was on the receiving end of a set of nun chucks being swung by Bruce Lee. One story finally made sense to me about the yogi and his student. Whenever the student asks about the key to enlightenment, the yogi, again and again, sends the student back to meditate. Who knows how long it takes for that student to understand that, as a human, he is the expression of what he continuously seeks. You can figure that out for yourself by turning inward, not in searching, but in surrender. Seekers often get so caught up in the act of searching that they miss the answer right before them. The more we focus on seeing the light in others the more it will show up prevalent in our own lives. It may seem like what I'm saying is a matter of semantics, but it's yet another delicate example of how the Universe responds to endless lookers, by continuously giving them something to look for. It's simple: just choose to see the best in others, and the best of us also comes forward.

The concept that we are all one is repeated often, but I wonder how people really perceive or experience this. It can be confusing to wrap our heads around the idea that everything is one because the individual human form leads us to believe we are separate. With the detailed buffet of emotions we have access to as humans, we could be led to believe that because we are different, we are separate. This sense of individuality results in a person feeling separate and alone, as I often did on my journey and during times of despair when I needed support. However, we are never truly alone in this persistent spiritual experience.

We often hear people say, "I want to become more spiritual, and more connected." There's no way to become more spiritually connected. We are a spirit born into a human form. We are what we seek. It's a matter of declaring the truth of who we are and understanding that there is nothing more to do, no action to take, it's just being. The presence of who we truly are has always existed and been there, even in times of tragedy and despair.

We don't remember we are spiritual beings having this human experience; we think we are humans occasionally having enlightened spiritual experiences. The opposite is true: each and every day, we are enlightened spirits having a human experience.

This idea was a lot to digest while reviewing my past and thinking of how these beautiful, disastrous heartbreaks crushed me and left me feeling broken and tired of life. It seemed like every time something crazy in my life was about to happen, I had a sense it was coming. The ground would rumble and much like when a tsunami is rolling up a big wave, there was no use in running. Something prevented me from running. How my life unfolded is a product of testing and trying these various trails, even the ones I knew would result in less than desirable outcomes. It isn't that I like going through heartache and pain, but I found that, each time, that pain became just another part of my human experience. I learned that it was okay to try or test out something else. In the beginning, my mind played funny games, telling me that things would turn out differently if I were better, stronger, prettier, or came from a different family. I wondered why love never seemed to work out for me. I believed in love, but struggled trying to understand what love was showing me. I asked these questions before understanding that we are in charge of what we bring to the table of life, much more than what we sometimes take responsibility for as humans.

How boring life would be if we experienced just one emotion all the time. What a gift it is to feel a wide range of emotions and to be able to love and accept them as they come.

Watch how young children find joy in nearly every daily task, and when they feel something else, they freely show that emotion too. Kids never fake what they are feeling inside. They are completely honest with their emotions. They haven't been told yet that their feelings and ideas are wrong.

As we grow up, our environment conditions us about which emotions we are free to express. We start to hide pieces of ourselves and begin to judge how others handle their emotions. This all runs counter to the way we came into being, with a divine sovereignty that says we can love and feel any way that we choose without the burden of social measures and standards laid upon us.

Everything here is to help us remember our own divinity. I believe this to be so with relationships, especially close relationships with lovers and immediate family. We attract what we need to learn, and so relationships can lead us to sail directly into our pain, which is sometimes why we might feel it coming. Oftentimes, relationships are gifts that give us the opportunity to face and resolve any pain that already exists within us, allowing us to continue to sail onward. It's a blessing really, but too often we forget to be grateful to the process because the human side of us is caught up in the emotional predicament and victim-hood of it all; blaming, pointing fingers, judging, and not truly loving the other without obligations (unconditionally, as we would hope to receive for our self). We lose our grace in these matters when we forget the fact that we are all just spirits that signed up to have this most excellent human adventure with each other and life. We aren't victims. We are never really victims of anything actually, because life doesn't occur out of contempt for us; life unfolds a magnificent tapestry of wisdom for us.

CHAPTER 17

Trust

"A bird sitting on a tree is never afraid of the branch breaking, because her trust is not on the branch, but on its own wings."

— Unknown

My life felt like a game of chutes and ladders invariably taking me back to the beginning of the game board, leading me to constantly revisit the approaches and perspectives in my life.

After my period of rest, I didn't return to working with clients right away; I still wasn't ready. Instead, I began writing. I came to a place where nothing in my life made sense anymore; not my work life, personal relationships, or healing work, and not those depended upon for spiritual guidance. It was time to focus and trust my own inner voice again, and not on the noise outside of me.

I felt an insistent and gentle nudge from within to begin writing a book. It was odd at first because even though I could feel the desire, my mind couldn't make sense of what to write or what I would be writing for. I had no idea how to write a book or get it published. As a cyber security professional, my experience didn't lend the same skill set to that of an author. The writing project began as a negotiation with the Universe, with me stating that I would begin writing but whether it turned into a book or got published was completely out of my hands. There was a voice inside of me that said, "Trust, and we will be with you every step of the way."

I shied away from writing about my life each time I sat down in front of the keyboard and attempted to begin. The days went by and I dragged my feet and pushed the task off to the side; finding a starting point seemed overwhelming. This was partly because I knew that, in this writing, I was going to have to be honest and allow myself to be vulnerable while talking about the twists and turns of my life. I would have to talk about my personal difficulties in a real way, which meant that the rest of me would be exposed, vulnerable, and open to scrutiny. The sides of me that I spent years hiding away, the emotional struggles, would be center stage.

I had always been hell bent on being successful and strong, and had always prevented anyone from seeing alternate aspects of myself. I'm not sure where I ever got the idea that it was required of me to be strong all the time. Maybe I had assumed this role the more times I felt let down by others and felt I could only count on myself. It could have been that one time in kindergarten on the playground where I had come to the defense of another girl being bullied and the older boy pushed me down to the ground, causing me to skin my knee, tear my tights, and soil my dress with mud. It was the last time I wore a dress to school. I remember silently deciding that dresses were limiting for me, and the tights left me feeling exposed. I was mad he got the best of me and felt powerless and weak in defending myself. Perhaps that's where I learned that I needed to be strong and be able to push back so I wouldn't be a victim. Maybe I took the strong girl on because I saw how people admired strength, heroes, and people who win, and I wanted to be regarded, respected, and admired in that way. Or perhaps I felt like if I ever showed sensitivity, tears, emotions, or vulnerability it would mean that I was a weak person who could easily be undone and couldn't handle her own life. Somewhere along the way, I decided to always be strong and not allow my vulnerability to be seen by anyone.

The downside of constantly standing in an armored suit is that it kept me from my own authenticity and it was a lot of work to constantly seal up the cracks in that armor. I realized and dealt with these things, but the idea of now sharing them with others terrified me so I pushed off the writing longer and longer. Even so, the gentle nagging continued to urge me to write.

Still in total avoidance of writing and busying myself with other tasks, I one day came across some old USB drives tossed in a box of miscellaneous items. Upon plugging them in to see if they could still be used, I discovered pages of my electronic journals that I had written and kept while living in the Middle East. Reading through the pages reminded me of all the emotions and thoughts I had experienced more than 15 years prior. It was interesting to reminisce back to those times, and to read my perspectives and points of view. It made me realize how much I had changed over the years. I started to understand more about how I used my path and passion for discovery through my professional assignments, travels, and even personal relationships. All I had been through seemed to point to today's understanding of myself, and my life. While reading through my writing, I began formatting and correcting sentences. Before I knew it, I was transferring and consolidating passages, and ending up with something that looked much like the beginnings of a book manuscript.

Over a period of a year I continued writing, filling in the missing pieces, and expanding the writing until I finally ended up with something that could possibly resemble a book. I still had no idea what to do next. Everyone had told me how hard it was to publish a book. After all, I wasn't even a real writer—I'm a cyber security engineer and a part-time energy healer. Who would be interested in my story? There was a lot of doubt and fear about sharing such intimate thoughts, feelings, and parts of my life that I hadn't even shared with my closest friends. Even my family had little knowledge about the details I was writing about. After all, I'd made a life out of being strong, secure, and eliminating any scent of vulnerability.

When the manuscript seemed finished, I just tipped my head back to the sky and said, "Here it is, the pieces of my life that have made me, me." There is the good, the bad, and everything in between, all the bits that I've worked hard to conceal and pieces that I worked hard to show. The cathartic learning and authentic pieces are all here. It may not be the most riveting or even interesting, but it is my story. It is the story of how I figured out my life, trusting the truth of who I am, learning to accept myself and stand fully in my decisions. That we should not be ashamed or in judgment of the things that make us human, and that we don't always need to be strong, nice, pretty, or have all the answers. In fact, the ones who can be weak, vulnerable, and stand eye-to-eye with fear are living in truth, not hiding. They aren't pretending to be strong, nor lying to himself or herself or the world about whom they are while advising others how they should be. It is not until we are willing to face everything, that we gain the full power of our selves.

Once I finished writing, I didn't want to look at it again. The rawness of uncomfortable feelings coursed through me. It didn't feel good at first, because I was still protecting the remnants of an image, but I'd been through much worse. I hung out with the idea that maybe no one would ever want to publish this book or think that it was good. And so what? My intuition had guided me to a task—to write the book—and so I did.

My overly neurotic sense about my writing ended as I emerged through a new emotional clearing, an open space in which I didn't have to live up my perfectionist expectations of myself. Accompanying that space was a lack of care or worry of criticism regarding my journey or perspectives.

I'm willing to be judged for following my heart, and for standing in my truth. The only thing I need to do is be true to who I am, to carry my message of inspiration and transformation to those who resonate with it, using my perspective, ideas, and experiences about my journey. Doing so can help show others how they could also discover and stand in their journeys, as opposed to constantly seeking external acceptance while standing in someone else's. If I'm judged, at least it will be for who I truly am, and I can live with that.

Days went by after I finished the manuscript and I grew busy helping my daughter transition from college to her first professional job after graduation. One day, I was speaking to the concierge in my apartment about having my daughter back home, how things seemed to come full circle with her staying at my house, and about the book I had written. He asked what the book was about and I gave him more details, how my life and my daughter's had started out in a small town and ended up with us traveling around the world. He was intrigued and said "Wow! I should introduce you to a friend of mine who has a publishing company. As a matter of fact, she lives in this building."

Astonished, I thought, it couldn't be that easy? I didn't even leave home. When trusting and following intuition, things do appear to unfold more easily. I reached out to the publisher and we scheduled a meeting. I described the details of my story, and after about an hour of my talking, I paused and asked her if she thought that the story could be good enough to be a book. She said she thought it might be, it sounded interesting; she asked me to send her the manuscript.

After the meeting, I went back to my apartment and felt nauseous. My daughter asked what was wrong. I described to her what had just happened. She said, "Wow, that seems really great. Why are you about to be sick?" Up until that point, I had just written and only talked about possibly publishing a book, and even pitched it to a publisher who liked the story. Now, someone was actually going to read what I had written; it just got real. I was a nervous wreck about sending the manuscript, with my finger hovering over the send button for a week. Was I ready to really walk this part of the journey? She might think I'm delusional, and what if this was the worst book ever written? Despite all my nerves, I finally sent the manuscript. This first version of the book needed a lot of work; it was just the beginning stages of my journey with writing. The editing and finished product would take another year to complete, and in the process of all the iterations and refinement of this text, I had even more realizations about myself and my journey.

The book you hold in your hands now is the result of that writing journey. I am a firm believer that when you stay in your heart and follow your intuition, you are, in a way, following the breadcrumbs life leaves for you each step you take along the way. The next step is often only revealed after the previous step has been fully taken, and it can happen in the most miraculous ways. After the injury, I found the healing work that led me to the warrior's rest. Following the truth of who I was led me to each next step, which brought me to begin writing. I had no idea how it would end up or unfold from there, but I reluctantly wrote anyway. Then, living five floors above me was the woman who would help publish my book? That was either a coincidence, or it was life unfolding for me because I was in the flow, following intuition and embracing the magic of uncertainty.

Throughout my journey, there have always been elements of uncertainty that have prompted me to let go of how I think things should happen. I'm consistently surprised that things just always seemed to show up right when I needed them. It requires a slight shift in focus on more of the *be*-ing aspect, rather than doing, and learning to trust uncertainty.

Writing was a great way for me to make sense of my journey. The writing led me to discover I had no regrets with how my life has unfolded or with the relationships, people, and so-called mentors that were left behind. Setting things down through writing was necessary for me to come into my own, to process my experiences and integrate what I learned into my life.

Life, to me, is the shortened version of the word Spirituality, and it isn't about trying to exist in perfection. It's about showing up and grabbing our experiences. Everyone is waking up and showing up every day, doing the best they can, taking their piece of this world one way or another. As time goes on, those pieces take shape and become the stories of our life. For better or worse, those experiences make us who we are. I don't think anyone should ever be afraid of what those experiences look like. The hard edges, bruises, the broken bits and pieces, even the dark stuff—it's all inherently relevant and every bit of it is beautiful. No one is ever judging us as hard as we are judging ourselves, and if they are, it's only because that's how they judge themselves while alone in their own mental garden.

If we ignore the dark corners because we are scared of what we might find, they will always be there to haunt us. There's no need to become obsessive about clearing the detritus out, but there's no need to be afraid to face it either. Once confronted, darkness stops having power over us and over our life decisions. The most brilliant and interesting people I've ever met in my life are full of scars inside and out. They've done their journeys while pushing the limits of their human potential without being ruled by fear or caring about other people's opinions. Instead, they were driven forward.

It's unfortunate when people feel the need to apologize for their scars and emotional turmoil. No one survives this journey unscathed, but then again, isn't that the point? There is no shame in experiencing or even talking about what's considered the less-than-fun stuff. Talk about it, tell your story, dive deep into that story and really feel all the emotion there is to feel, without judgment. Diving into that is also a spiritual experience to have, if that is what is chosen. Whatever happens, we shouldn't ever just dance around the edge of the water, only ever so slightly dipping in a toe. When we do that, resistance builds in response to our avoidance (what you resist, persists). If we get overly compulsive about clearing away our negative past, we only succeed in digging up more problems. The Universe obliges, helping to find more to dig up, continuously producing more and more to be cleared away, over and over again. The fact that an emotion or painful memory is coming up doesn't necessarily mean that there is something unbalanced, unwholesome, or wrong within us. The process is proof of an evolving spirit. Let it be that, without feeling a need to fix something.

Everything I thought I knew about life was amiss, and becoming a healer turned my world upside down. It taught me that knowledge and learning could be refuted by a higher truth. Even today when I think I have a handle on something, that concept gets shattered as well. Then a new possibility turns up, informing me that things aren't black and white, but can co-exist as truths in different ways.

I got some big lessons about trusting myself. I no longer needed to look to others for my answers or approval. In fact, I stopped looking altogether because whatever I need comes naturally when I'm patient. That's the divine order of things. By writing down my thoughts and feelings, and listening to the soft words of my soul—whether in the quietest or most hectic moments—I now hear a voice of trust and life shows up to dance with me much differently.

We all know how every life story ends. The interesting part is the surprise in the middle. So the message is to stop stressing out about the outcome and just enjoy the middle parts. What's meant for us will always find us no matter which path we take.

There were periods of my life that I felt that by doing what I was doing in my professional career, perhaps I wasn't on my "spiritual path." Was my professional career being used to avoid my personal truths and spiritual purpose? Perhaps, secretly I feared who I really was, and felt there was less risk of making mistakes and failing if I stayed within the boundaries of what had become familiar and comfortable.

In the midst of all the efforts I made to create my own security, my purpose was still found, even after times when I felt the train went off the tracks in terms of being in alignment with my life purpose. In the end, I needed to fearlessly face my own vulnerability in order to tap into my true self. I had to see myself as a divine expression and learn how to acknowledge this truth in my everyday living. After years of feeling the need to always be so strong and together, maybe subconsciously I was drawn to finding vulnerability professionally because that's what was needed most in my life to recreate balance. Whatever it was, the answers to the questions I was asking were right under my nose all along.

Our creations can lead us to unsavory situations that bring with them an incredible amount of guilt at times. When I was lying flat on my back in Paris after being injured in the fall, I had some really deep reflections about the way I was living and saw the aspects of myself that I hadn't been willing to face. Ultimately, my injury became a life-changing event. It was painful but it served a purpose, yet another rite of passage. It put me on the path of transformational healing and of becoming a healer in my own right, which got me to slow down and see life differently. The healing work allowed me to release the guilt I felt for past decisions that were made, and for living without being grateful. It essentially led me back to my love for life. Maybe, on some level, I did create the situation, or maybe it was the only way that the Universe could slow me down to get my attention.

My life has taught me how to hold the space of truth for others when they cannot muster that love or recognition for themselves. When life becomes difficult for us, we are less able to respond with grace and kindness. Handling difficult situations with grace is a talent, like learning to be a healer, a skill that sometimes, too, must be cultivated. Some days I handle difficult situations well, and not as well on other days. None of this work has made me perfect, but it has made me more aware and sensitive to choices and responses that are made. No one ever said that spiritually was supposed to be pretty.

There probably is not a path to higher consciousness and enlightenment where unicorns and rainbows reside. Okay, maybe there is, but if so, it would probably be found by turning inward, not in the eyes and mind of another. You are a perfect divine expression of all that is. Another big surprise on this journey is the fact that there isn't a path to higher consciousness that does not lead you back to deal with yourself.

I'm humbled by the people I've had the opportunity to serve, especially the ones I've been able to lay my hands on. The opportunity to touch, serve, and help others in their lives is an amazing gift. For that I'll always be grateful. I only have a little more understanding or additional explanation of how this all works today than I did the very first day I started. What I have gained is a respect for the inherent healing nature of the human body and the resilience of the human spirit that continues to faithfully shine even in our darkest of moments. There's a deep appreciation for the perfection and magnificence of the vessel where all of our spirits reside.

CHAPTER 18

Reflections

"Maybe the journey isn't so much about becoming anything. Maybe it's about un-becoming everything that isn't really you so you can be who you were meant to be in the first place."

— Unknown

When I reflect back on the events in my life, I celebrate the great times and magnificent journey. In many ways, my journey was difficult and oftentimes confusing. I was always expecting something to feel finished, giving me a feeling of completeness or a bigger sense of satisfaction. I often thought, "Shouldn't there be a feeling of exhilaration inside of me? I'm in a new place and it's exotic, beautiful, and different, so I should feel differently, right?" Constantly going from one thing to the next, I somehow expected it to give me something more internally. No matter where I tried to escape to, there was no escaping me. My knowledge grew about cultures and places, but there was no ah-ha moment or great realness in any one of those places or people that made me feel okay. It took me a long time to see that the drive and curiosity that sent me all over the world was a piece of me that was hoping to discover me.

I began this journey to pursue a better life for myself and my daughter. Along the way, I discovered my way forward in life, although not in a conventional way. I made the difficult decision not to become a full time parent to my daughter. At that time, her father was better able to assume those responsibilities. It took me a while to make peace with this arrangement, but it was the right decision for Jordan and, rather than harm our relationship, over time we became closer. My work and travels provided my daughter with a dynamic upbringing and the opportunity to see many parts of the world. While her dad and other mother provided a stable home, I was her example of what else was possible for a woman to achieve. Today, Jordan values that she has lived a diverse life, seeing both sides of the traditional and non-traditional roles of a family. "I've had the best of both worlds," she tells me. Now she gets to choose what will work best for her and in her family in the future.

The story of my life includes many disastrous love stories. Over the period of 20 years, I have indeed learned a lot of lessons about love and love lost. However, the most important love story is the love and acceptance I eventually found within myself. Without the perceived disasters of the past, I might not be experiencing a kinder, wiser, and more loving self today. It may have taken all that turmoil, adventure, and sense of wonder to wake me up to the recognition of myself. Otherwise I might still be running around from one job, country, or relationship to the next, standing so strong and never truly facing any of what comes with living out the human experience.

Reaching the top of each mountain peak on the trail of life isn't the best or most exciting part of the journey. The best and most exciting part of the journey is the trail walking itself, the excitement and anticipation, the exploration, the learning, and the remembering of who we are along the way. How boring would life be if there was nothing interesting along the way up the mountain? Imagine that the journey consisted only of a white ceiling, white walls, and a white floor, and that we walked for days and days, maybe up a few white stairs, before finally reaching the top. Well, the top isn't so sweet when we haven't seen and experienced interesting things or overcome anything along the path. If we didn't learn or recognize who we truly are or find anything new on that path, then the path looking down the mountain would certainly look a bit boring and unmemorable.

The more exciting path is lush with exotic green trees, flowers, and evergreens. It has winding trails and switchbacks, curves and cliffs and even pitfalls that require a bit of skill to navigate or come across safely. Maybe there's even a bear or lion that crosses the path. Do you decide to pause, take on a challenge, or do you run for your life? Maybe the path is full of exotic birds and creatures and every step of the journey up the path is an expedition of discovery to a whole new you and a whole new way that's never been seen or encountered. Then the rain comes and shelter is needed, days and nights grow cold and dark for a while. After some time, the sun shines and again you pause and rest awhile so the warmth of the rays bounces off your skin and begins to soothe you down to your bones. Continuing up the path, looking across the horizon, you can see the beginning of the winding path through the valley and up the mountain. You remember the encounter with the bear, and reflect on your expert survival skills. You remember the stream and the chirping birds that guided you to beautiful patches of exotic fruits. Looking back through everything you survived, you did so with triumph and pride, and you enjoyed most of your journey. You can reflect back on how clever and strong you could be when it was needed, when it really mattered most.

No matter how unhappy or unfulfilled we think our lives are, we can take a pause and look at the journey and how beautiful it is along the way. Life wouldn't be as sweet, interesting, or fulfilling walking down a plain white hallway to immediately arrive at every desired destination. Learning to love and appreciate the way life unfolds for us, no matter how far we traveled or what we achieved or learned along the way, is the biggest gift of self-acceptance we can give ourselves.

The result of my journey is that I like and value myself more than I ever have. This value is with less ego and unbalanced selfishness, and with more levels of kindness toward myself. After setting aside the professional ladder that I was feverishly climbing in an effort to better define a sense of belonging for myself, I took a moment to pause. This pause and review was about healing and becoming a healer, and after that, figuring out who else could I be in this life?

My healing work with clients and family members continues. While I enjoy helping others, I also enjoy spending time with my daughter, doing speaking engagements, writing, running workshops, and exploring other aspects of life. Healing work also taught me that in life things aren't always black or white, nor are they an all-or-nothing proposition. It's about blending and balancing together our life's joys, while we flow with our intuition, passion, curiosity, and interest. It's about being willing to be led down many paths and being open to endless possibilities. Being a healer isn't how my story ends; it is an exciting new beginning of a most excellent adventure, leading me to endless prospects for life's adventures.

My wish in writing this book is that it will inspire people to stand in their truth, own their character, expand perspectives, or maybe help soothe them on a difficult path in their lives. It would help them navigate and expand broader ways to finding their peace, or perhaps, during a difficult moment, reassure them that everything would be okay. Things are always going to be okay, even when it feels that they aren't.

Finally, in all this wondering and exploration I've found it useful to trade in my map for a compass, so to speak. I don't think we have to go through life following the path of those who have gone before. And we don't need to know the exact route of where life is taking us. We just need to have an idea of a general direction, faith in our truth, and a willingness to go forward.

Resources:

Contact Information: Darcy@darcyhotchkiss.com

Acknowledgements

Much thanks goes to my daughter, Jordan, who patiently supported me as I went through the process of writing this book. Appreciation and gratitude goes out to my friends and family, as well as my C4 family, who kept me motivated and believed in me. Your support means so much to me.

Special thanks to Ian Palmer, Cathie Lindsey, Stephanie Clearwater, and Dr. Lynn Joseph for your input, clarity, and sage advice that really helped bring things together in a big way.

Thank you to my teacher and friend, Zoran Hochstatter, for helping to transform my life and teaching me a whole new way to go to the beach.

Last but not least, thank you from the bottom of my heart to Selven Watts, who one day was moved to make an important introduction between me and Charlene Giannetti at Wat-Age Publishing. Without her advice, this book would not be what it is today. I am humbled by what I have learned and realized during this process, and am grateful to share my story. So a big heartfelt thank you.

About the Author

Darcy Hotchkiss is a U.S. Army veteran and has spent the last 17 years working in various assignments for the Department of Defense around the world. She has also had an unquenchable curiosity in personal development and alterative healing approaches. She grew up in Oakland, Maine but now calls Arlington, Virginia home.

Photo credit: Tamzin B. Smith Portrait Photography